Æsop's Fables

ÆSOP'S FABLES

Illustrated Junior Library®

WITH DRAWINGS BY Fritz Kredel

GROSSET & DUNLAP ❧ *Publishers*

PRINTED ON RECYCLED PAPER

Copyright 1947 by Grosset & Dunlap, Inc.
Copyright renewal 1975 by Grosset & Dunlap, Inc. All rights reserved.
Published by Grosset & Dunlap, Inc., a member of
Penguin Putnam Books for Young Readers, New York.
Published simultaneously in Canada.
Printed in the United States of America.
GROSSET & DUNLAP is a trademark of Grosset & Dunlap, Inc.
Illustrated Junior Library is a registered trademark of Grosset & Dunlap, Inc.
Library of Congress Catalog Card Number: 47-27068   ISBN 0-448-06003-5

2000 Printing

The FABLES

THE LIFE AND WORK OF AESOP

SOMETIME between the years 620 and 560 B.C. there came to the court of Croesus, last of the kings of Lydia in Asia Minor, a freedman known as Aesop. While still a slave of Iadmon on the island of Samos he had gained some local fame for himself and considerable prestige for his master as a narrator of tales about animals.

At any rate, the ex-slave's renown had preceded him when he arrived at Sardis to match wits with such exiled pundits as Solon of Athens and Thales of Miletus and the other sages and philosophers who had gathered at the court of the outstanding patron of learning of that time. There is no doubt that the former bondsman quickly grew in favor with Croesus as a result of his shrewd intelligence and native wit, plus a certain amount of well-directed flattery. It would be a mistake, however, to look upon Aesop as a sort of court jester, for while he came to amuse he remained to instruct, and Croesus probably learned more home truths from his fables than from all the serious disquisitions of the royal stable of philosophers.

In time, as the King acquired what amounted to practically a hegemony over the other small Greek states, Aesop began to be employed as an ambassador to the various capitals. In this capacity his shrewd use of the beast tales, or fables, stood him in good stead. At Corinth he warned his hearers against mob law in a fable, later used by Socrates. At Athens by the recital of *The Frogs Desiring a King* he warned the citizenry that the known tyranny of Pisistratus might be preferable to that of an unknown successor.

His visit to Delphi seems to have had less of a political objective. It was to cost him his life. Sent as a commissioner by Croesus to distribute some payment due the Delphians, he incurred the displeasure of the inhabitants of that important city. The story goes that as he was ready to leave on his homeward journey to Sardis, a gold cup from the temple of Apollo was found in his baggage where it had been planted. Charged with impiety and sacrilege, Aesop was brought to trial. For once his ready weapon failed to serve him. He is said to have appealed to the Delphian reverence for the laws of hospitality with the fable of *The Eagle and the Beetle*, but he appealed in vain. The enraged guardians of the temple, feeling, perhaps, that their sinecure might be in danger, condemned the ambassador of Croesus to be hurled to his death from a high cliff outside the city.

We are told that the conscience-smitten Delphians lived to regret the violent death of Aesop. After a succession of disasters the harried citizenry offered reparation for the envoy's death. It was awarded to the grandson of Iadmon, Aesop's old master. The proverb of "Aesop's blood" in aftertimes gave warning to his countrymen that a murdered man's blood will not cry to heaven in vain.

But the fame of Aesop lived on. About two hundred years after his death his statue, carved by Lysippus, was erected at Athens, and it was placed in front of the statues of the Seven Sages.

We know that Aesop never wrote down any of his fables, and we know, also, that the first recorded compilation of the tales that bear his name was not made until nearly three centuries after his death, but for generations it was deemed an indispensable accomplishment of an Athenian gentleman to be able to tell a good story of Aesop's at the club. His practical wisdom was as highly regarded as his caustic humor. The common tradition that he appeared alive again and fought at Thermopylae speaks more for the honor in which he was held as a patriot than a hundred more plausible anecdotes could do.

Did Aesop invent the fable? No. He merely used a form of the beast tale whose origin can be traced back to many Eastern nations. It was natural among primitive people to compare human motives and acts with the ways of the wily fox, the timid deer, and the noble lion. It followed that the animals of forest and barnyard should be endowed with human passions and feelings, and even with human speech. The fable in those early times was not a child's plaything. It was a nation's primer.

In Greece, during the times of the Tyrants, when free speech was dangerous, the fable began to be used for political purposes. It was in this field that Aesop developed the ancient beast tale which flourished in India long before. When neither kings nor mobs could be made to look upon the naked truth, Aesop found that this style of primitive wisdom furnished an effective garb with which to clothe it. Tyranny and rebellion alike were stayed by this offhand, ready-made weapon of the man of action who united presence of mind with presence of wit. Even when free speech was established among the Hellenic democracies the custom of using fables in serious public orations as well as lighter after-dinner speeches continued.

About three centuries after Aesop's time Demetrius Phalereus of Athens, founder of the Alexandria Library, collected the fables he could find under the title *Assemblies of Aesopic Tales*. There were about two hundred fables in the compilation. Later, a Greek freedman of Augustus Caesar, named Phaedrus, in the early years of the Christian era turned them into Latin iambics. Later still, in the time of Marcus Aurelius, Valerius Babrius, a tutor to the young son of Alexander Severus, merged with the Aesopic fables a collection of Indian, or Libyan, beast tales. In the 1300's, a monk of Constantinople, named Maximus Planudes, compiled a definitive book of fables. Each collector and each translator added and changed and edited and inserted. From all these various sources the bulk of the existing fables is derived. All the anachronisms, the mixtures of pagan and Christian forms of speech and sentiment, are indications of the many hands through which the original fables, many of which had their origin in ancient India, passed.

Despite the wear and tear of twenty-five centuries, the spirit and the body of Aesop's fables are still intact, if not as they proceeded from the lips of the ex-slave in the court of Croesus, at least as they were known in the best times of Greek literature.

THE DOG IN THE MANGER

A DOG looking for a quiet and comfortable place to take a nap jumped into the manger of the ox and lay there on the hay.

Some time later the ox, returning hungry from his day's work, entered his stall and found the dog in his manger. The dog, in a rage because he had been awakened from his nap, stood up and barked and snapped whenever the ox came near his hay.

The ox is a patient beast, but finally he protested: "Dog, if you wanted to eat my dinner I would have no objection. But you will neither eat it yourself nor let me enjoy it, which strikes me as a very churlish way to act."

Application: SOME BEGRUDGE OTHERS WHAT THEY CANNOT ENJOY THEMSELVES.

1

THE WOLF IN SHEEP'S CLOTHING

A WOLF had been lurking near a flock of sheep for several days. But so vigilant had been the shepherd in guarding his animals that the wolf was becoming desperate.

Then one day the wolf found a sheepskin that had been thrown away. Quickly he slipped it on over his own hide and made his way among the flock of grazing sheep. Even the shepherd was deceived by the ruse, and when night came the wolf in his disguise was shut up with the sheep in the fold.

But that evening the shepherd, wanting something for his supper, went down to the fold, and reaching in, seized the first animal he came to. Mistaking the wolf for a sheep the shepherd killed him on the spot.

ᒊᐛ *Application:* APPEARANCES OFTEN ARE DECEIVING.

2

MERCURY AND THE
WOODMAN

AN HONEST, hard-working woodman was fell-ing a tree on the bank of a deep river. In some way his hand slipped and his ax fell into the water and immediately sank to the bottom. Being a poor man who could ill afford to lose the tool by which he earned his livelihood he sat down and lamented his loss most bitterly.

But Mercury, whose river it was, suddenly ap-peared on the scene. When he had learned of the woodman's misfortune, he offered to do what he could to help.

Diving into the deep, swift-flowing stream, he brought up an ax made of solid gold.

"Could this be yours?" he asked.

"Alas, I wish it were," replied the woodman sadly.

Again Mercury dived into the icy-cold water and this time brought up an ax made of solid silver. But again the woodman shook his head and denied that the tool belonged to him. Mercury dived a third time and produced the identical ax which the man had lost.

Naturally the owner was delighted to see his trusty ax once more, and so was Mercury.

"You are an honest and a good man," said the messenger of the gods. "I want you to take the golden and the silver ax as a reward for telling the truth."

Thanking his benefactor, the woodman ran home to tell his wife of his good fortune. As the story spread, one of the neighbors rushed down to the same spot on the riverbank, threw his ax into the water, and began to moan and groan over his loss. Just as before, Mercury appeared, and learning what had occurred, dived into the water and fetched up a golden ax.

"Is this the ax you lost, my friend?" he asked.

"Yes, yes, that's it," lied the man, greedily reaching for the golden ax in Mercury's hand. But just as he was about to grasp the ax of gold, Mercury said: "Not so fast, sir. You are lying, and to punish you for not being truthful, I am not only denying you this, but I am leaving your own ax at the bottom of the river."

ઠ⊷ *Application*: HONESTY IS THE BEST POLICY.

THE FOX AND
THE CROW

ε≫ A CROW who had stolen a piece of cheese was flying toward the top of a tall tree where he hoped to enjoy his prize, when a fox spied him. "If I plan this right," said the fox to himself, "I shall have cheese for supper."

So, as he sat under the tree, he began to speak in his politest tones: "Good day, mistress crow, how well you are looking today! How glossy your wings, and your breast is the breast of an eagle. And your claws—I beg pardon—your talons are as strong as steel. I have not heard your voice, but I am certain that it must surpass that of any other bird just as your beauty does."

The vain crow was pleased by all this flattery. She believed every word of it and waggled her tail and flapped her wings to show her pleasure. She liked especially what friend fox said about her voice, for she had sometimes been told that her caw was a bit rusty. So, chuckling to think how she was going to surprise the fox with her most beautiful caw, she opened wide her mouth.

Down dropped the piece of cheese! The wily fox snatched it before it touched the ground, and as he walked away, licking his chops, he offered these words of advice to the silly crow: "The next time someone praises your beauty be sure to hold your tongue."

“➤ *Application*: FLATTERERS ARE NOT TO BE TRUSTED.

THE GARDENER AND
HIS DOG

THE GARDENER was drawing water at the well to water his garden plants. His little dog was jumping and barking on the well curb until he lost his balance and fell in.

Hearing the splash, the gardener quickly drew off his clothes and descended into the well to rescue his dog. Just as he was bringing the struggling and slippery animal to the top, the ungrateful wretch bit his master's hand.

"Why, you little monster," exclaimed the gardener. "If that is your idea of gratitude to a master who feeds you and pets you and treats you kindly, then pull yourself out of the well." With that he dropped the dog right back into the well again.

&❧ *Application*: DON'T BITE THE HAND THAT FEEDS YOU!

7

THE ANGLER
AND THE LITTLE FISH

༭ AN ANGLER after a long day's toil, had nothing to show for his pains but one small fish. As he was taking the perch off the hook the fish spoke:

"Spare me, good fisherman. I am so small that I will make you but a sorry meal. Throw me back into the river, and later when I am grown bigger and worth eating, you may come here and catch me again."

"No, no," said the wary angler, "I have you now, but if you once get back into the water, your tune will be 'catch me if you can.'"

༭ *Application*: BEWARE OF THE PROMISES OF A DES-
PERATE MAN!

THE FAWN AND HER MOTHER

ONE DAY in the forest a fawn was browsing among some ferns with her mother. It was peaceful there in the shelter of the forest growth. Suddenly, from a distance came the sound of baying hounds. The mother deer stood stock-still and began to tremble.

"Mother," said the fawn, "you are bigger than a dog and swifter of foot and better winded, and you have horns with which to defend yourself. Why are you so afraid of the hounds?"

The mother smiled, and said: "All this, my child, I know full well. But no sooner do I hear a dog bark than, somehow or other, my heels take me off as fast as they can carry me."

Application: THERE IS NO ARGUING A COWARD INTO COURAGE.

9

THE MILKMAID AND
HER PAIL

A MILKMAID was on her way to market, carrying a pail of milk on the top of her head. As she walked along the road in the early morning she began to turn over in her mind what she would do with the money she would receive for the milk.

"I shall buy some hens from a neighbor," said she to herself, "and they will lay eggs every day which I shall sell to the pastor's wife. And with the egg money I'll buy myself a new frock and ribbon. Green they should be, for green becomes my complexion best. And in this lovely green gown I will go to the fair. All the young men will strive to have me for a partner. I shall pretend that I do not see them. When they become too insistent I shall disdainfully toss my head—like this."

As the milkmaid spoke she tossed her head back, and down came the pail of milk, spilling all over the

10

ground. And so all her imaginary happiness vanished, and nothing was left but an empty pail and the promise of a scolding when she returned home.

ℰ◢ *Application*: DO NOT COUNT YOUR CHICKENS BEFORE THEY ARE HATCHED.

THE ANT AND
THE GRASSHOPPER

ONE FROSTY autumn day an ant was busily storing away some of the kernels of wheat which he had gathered during the summer to tide him over the coming winter.

A grasshopper, half perishing from hunger, came limping by. Perceiving what the industrious ant was doing, he asked for a morsel from the ant's store to save his life.

"What were you doing all during the summer while I was busy harvesting?" inquired the ant.

"Oh," replied the grasshopper, "I was not idle. I was singing and chirping all day long."

"Well," said the ant, smiling grimly as he locked his granary door, "since you sang all summer, it looks as though you would have to dance all winter."

Application: IT IS THRIFTY TO PREPARE TODAY FOR THE WANTS OF TOMORROW.

THE MICE IN
COUNCIL

;ʜ FOR MANY YEARS the mice had been living in constant dread of their enemy, the cat. It was decided to call a meeting to determine the best means of handling the situation. Many plans were discussed and rejected.

At last a young mouse got up. "I propose," said he, looking very important, "that a bell be hung around the cat's neck. Then whenever the cat approaches, we always shall have notice of her presence, and so be able to escape."

The young mouse sat down amidst tremendous applause. The suggestion was put to a motion and passed almost unanimously.

But just then an old mouse, who had sat silent all the while, rose to his feet and said: "My friends, it takes a young mouse to think of a plan so ingenious and yet so simple. With a bell about the cat's neck to warn us we shall all be safe. I have but one brief question to put to the supporters of the plan—which one of you is going to bell the cat?"

;ʜ *Application*: IT IS ONE THING TO PROPOSE, AN-
OTHER TO EXECUTE.

13

THE GNAT
AND THE BULL

ONCE THERE WAS a silly gnat who kept buzzing about the head of a bull. Finally he settled himself down upon one of the bull's horns.

"Pardon me, Mr. Bull," he said, "if I am inconveniencing you. If my weight in any way is burdensome to you, pray say so, and I will be off in a moment."

"Oh, never trouble your head about that," replied the bull. "It is all the same to me whether you go or stay. To tell you the truth, I was not even aware that you were there."

Application: THE SMALLER THE MIND THE GREATER THE CONCEIT.

THE FOX AND
THE GOAT

ଏ A FOX had the misfortune to fall into a well from which, try as he might, he could not escape. Just as he was beginning to be worried a goat came along intent on quenching his thirst.

"Why, friend fox, what are you doing down there?" he cried.

"Do you mean to say that you haven't heard about the great drought, friend goat?" the fox said. "Just as soon as I heard I jumped down here where the water is plentiful. I would advise you to come down, too. It is the best water I have ever tasted. I have drunk so much that I can scarcely move."

When the goat heard this he leaped into the well without any more ado. The fox immediately jumped to the goat's back and using her long horns was able to scramble out of the well to safety. Then he called down to the unhappy goat the following advice: "The next time, friend goat, be sure to look before you leap!"

ଏ *Application*: IT IS NOT SAFE TO TRUST THE ADVICE OF A MAN IN DIFFICULTIES.

15

THE ASS CARRYING

SALT

⇌ THE RUMOR reached a certain huckster who owned an ass that salt was to be had cheap at the seaside. So he and the ass proceeded down to the shore to buy some. There he loaded his poor beast with as much as he could bear and started for home. As they were passing a slippery ledge of rock, the sorely laden ass fell into the stream below. The water melted the salt, thus relieving the beast of his burden. Gaining the bank with ease, he pursued his journey homeward light in body and in spirit.

The huckster, nothing daunted, set out again for the seashore for a load of salt. He piled an even heavier burden upon the ass. On their return, as they crossed the stream into which the ass previously had fallen by accident, this time he fell down on purpose. As before, the water dissolved the salt and freed him from his load.

Very much provoked by his loss, the master began to think how he could cure the animal of his tricks. So, on the next journey to the seacoast he freighted the ass with a load of sponges. When they arrived at

16

the same stream as before the beast was up to his old tricks once more. No sooner was he in the river than the sponges became soaked with water, and instead of lightening his burden, he found as he staggered homeward that he had more than doubled the weight of it.

℘ *Application*: AN OLD TRICK MAY BE PLAYED ONCE TOO OFTEN.

17

THE FOX AND THE
GRAPES

MISTER FOX was just about famished, and thirsty too, when he stole into a vineyard where the sun-ripened grapes were hanging up on a trellis in a tempting show, but too high for him to reach. He took a run and a jump, snapping at the nearest bunch, but missed. Again and again he jumped, only to miss the luscious prize. At last, worn out with his efforts, he retreated, muttering: "Well, I never really wanted those grapes anyway. I am sure they are sour, and perhaps wormy in the bargain."

Application: ANY FOOL CAN DESPISE WHAT HE CANNOT GET.

THE HARE
WITH MANY FRIENDS

ॐ THERE WAS ONCE a hare who had so many friends in the forest and the field that she truly felt herself to be the most popular member of the animal kingdom. One day she heard the hounds approaching.

"Why should a popular creature like me have to run for her life every time she hears a dog?" said she to herself. So she went to the horse, and asked him to carry her away from the hounds on his back.

"There is nothing I would rather do, friend hare," said the horse, "but, unfortunately, right now I have some important work to do for my master. However, a popular creature like you should have no difficulty in getting someone to help you."

Then the hare went to the bull and asked him whether he would be kind enough to ward off the hounds with his horns.

"My dear friend," replied the bull, "you know how I feel about you, and how glad I always am to be of service. But at this very moment I have an appointment with a lady. Why don't you ask our mutual friend the goat?"

But the goat was busy too, and so was the ram, and so were the calf and the pig and the ass. Each assured the hare of his undying friendship and anxiety to aid her in her trouble, but each had some excuse which prevented him from performing the service. By this time the hounds were quite near, so the hare took to her heels and luckily escaped.

ಌ *Application*: HE WHO HAS MANY FRIENDS HAS NO FRIENDS.

20

THE HARE
AND THE HOUND

ONE DAY a hound, out hunting by himself, flushed a hare from a thicket and gave chase. The frightened hare gave the dog a long run and escaped. As the disappointed hound turned back toward home, a passing goatherd said jeeringly: "You are a fine hunter! Aren't you ashamed to let a little hare one-tenth your size give you the best of it?"

"You forget," replied the hound, "that I was only running for my supper, but the hare was running for his life!"

ౘ❧ *Application*: NECESSITY IS OUR STRONGEST
WEAPON.

THE HOUSE DOG
AND THE WOLF

THE MOON was shining very bright one night when a lean, half-starved wolf, whose ribs were almost sticking through his skin, chanced to meet a plump, well-fed house dog. After the first compliments had been passed between them, the wolf inquired:

"How is it, cousin dog, that you look so sleek and contented? Try as I may I can barely find enough food to keep me from starvation."

"Alas, cousin wolf," said the house dog, "you lead too irregular a life. Why do you not work steadily as I do?"

"I would gladly work steadily if I could only get a place," said the wolf.

"That's easy," replied the dog. "Come with me to my master's house and help me keep the thieves away at night."

"Gladly," said the wolf, "for as I am living in the

woods I am having a sorry time of it. There is nothing like having a roof over one's head and a bellyful of victuals always at hand."

"Follow me," said the dog.

While they were trotting along together the wolf spied a mark on the dog's neck. Out of curiosity he could not forbear asking what had caused it.

"Oh, that's nothing much," replied the dog. "Perhaps my collar was a little tight, the collar to which my chain is fastened—"

"Chain!" cried the wolf in surprise. "You don't mean to tell me that you are not free to rove where you please?"

"Why, not exactly," said the dog, somewhat shamefacedly. "You see, my master thinks I am a bit fierce, and ties me up in the daytime. But he lets me run free at night. It really is very convenient for everybody. I get plenty of sleep during the day so that I can watch better at night. I really am a great favorite at the house. The master feeds me off his own plate, and the servants are continually offering me handouts from the kitchen. But wait, where are you going?"

As the wolf started back toward the forest he said: "Good night to you, my poor friend, you are welcome to your dainties—and your chains. As for me, I prefer my freedom to your fat."

$\approx$ *Application*: LEAN FREEDOM IS BETTER THAN FAT SLAVERY.

THE GOOSE WITH
THE GOLDEN EGGS

A FARMER went to the nest of his goose to see whether she had laid an egg. To his surprise he found, instead of an ordinary goose egg, an egg of solid gold. Seizing the golden egg he rushed to the house in great excitement to show it to his wife.

Every day thereafter the goose laid an egg of pure gold. But as the farmer grew rich he grew greedy. And thinking that if he killed the goose he could have all her treasure at once, he cut her open only to find —nothing at all.

Application: THE GREEDY WHO WANT MORE LOSE ALL.

THE FOX AND
THE HEDGEHOG

ও◆ A FOX in some unaccountable fashion got his tail entangled in a thicket which held him as closely as though he had been caught in a trap. In no time at all myriads of mosquitoes, seeing his plight, settled down upon him to enjoy a good meal undisturbed by his brush.

A hedgehog who chanced to be strolling by felt sorry for the fox and approached him, saying:

"Friend fox, you seem to be in a most unfortunate situation. Would you like me to make you more comfortable by driving off these bloodsucking pests?"

But to the hedgehog's surprise the fox replied: "No; thank you, my good friend, but I beg you not to disturb them."

"And why not?" persisted the well-meaning hedgehog.

"Well, you see," replied the fox, "these mosquitoes which you see have already drawn their fill of blood. If you chase them away a fresh swarm of hungry ones will descend upon me and they will not leave a drop of blood in my body."

ૐ *Application*: A NEEDY THIEF STEALS MORE THAN ONE WHO ENJOYS PLENTY.

27

THE HORSE AND
THE STAG

A BITTER QUARREL arose between the horse and the stag in the days when both creatures roamed wild in the forest. The horse came to the hunter to ask him to take his side in the feud.

The hunter agreed, but added: "If I am to help you punish the stag, you must let me place this iron bit in your mouth and this saddle upon your back."

The horse was agreeable to the man's conditions and he soon was bridled and saddled. The hunter sprang into the saddle, and together they soon had put the stag to flight. When they returned, the horse said to the hunter: "Now if you will get off my back and remove the bit and the saddle, I won't require your help any longer."

28

"Not so fast, friend horse," replied the hunter. "I have you under bit and spur, and from now on you shall remain the slave of man."

⅋ *Application*: LIBERTY IS TOO HIGH A PRICE TO PAY FOR REVENGE.

THE LION AND
THE BULLS

A LION often prowled about a pasture where three bulls grazed together. He had tried without success to lure one or the other of them to the edge of the pasture. He had even attempted a direct attack, only to see them form a ring so that from whatever direction he approached he was met by the horns of one of them.

Then a plan began to form in the lion's mind. Secretly he started spreading evil and slanderous reports of one bull against the other. The three bulls, distrustingly, began to avoid one another, and each withdrew to a different part of the pasture to graze. Of course, this was exactly what the lion wanted. One by one he fell upon the bulls, and so made easy prey of them all.

Application: UNITED WE STAND; DIVIDED WE FALL.

THE GOATHERD
AND THE GOATS

ॐ ONE WINTER'S DAY when the wind was blowing a gale and the snow was falling fast, a goatherd drove his goats, all white with snow, into a near-by cave for shelter. To his surprise, the goatherd found the cave already occupied by a herd of wild goats more numerous than his own.

The greedy man, thinking to secure them all, left his own goats to take care of themselves while he threw the branches which he had brought for them to the wild goats for fodder.

When the weather cleared, alas, the goatherd found that his own goats had perished from hunger, while the wild goats were off and away to the hills and woods. The foolish man returned a laughing-stock to his neighbors, for he not only had failed to gain the herd of wild goats, but he had lost his own.

ॐ *Application*: THEY WHO NEGLECT THEIR OLD FRIENDS FOR THE SAKE OF NEW ONES ARE RIGHTLY SERVED WHEN THEY LOSE BOTH.

31

THE HARE AND
THE TORTOISE

A HARE was continually poking fun at a tortoise because of the slowness of his pace. The tortoise tried not to be annoyed by the jeers of the hare, but one day in the presence of the other animals he was goaded into challenging the hare to a foot race.

"Why, this is a joke," said the hare. "You know that I can run circles around you."

"Enough of your boasting," said the tortoise. "Let's get on with the race."

So the course was set by the animals, and the fox was chosen as judge. He gave a sharp bark and the race was on. Almost before you could say "scat" the hare was out of sight. The tortoise plodded along at his usual unhurried pace.

After a time the hare stopped to wait for the tortoise to come along. He waited for a long, long time until he began to get sleepy. "I'll just take a quick nap here in this soft grass, and then in the cool of the day I'll finish the race." So he lay down and closed his eyes.

Meanwhile, the tortoise plodded on. He passed the sleeping hare, and was approaching the finish line when the hare awoke with a start. It was too late to save the race. Much ashamed, he crept away while all the animals at the finish line acclaimed the winner.

ુ Application: SLOW AND STEADY WINS THE RACE.

33

ANDROCLES AND
THE LION

⟨꙰⟩ ONCE THERE was a slave named Androcles who was cruelly treated by his master. When the opportunity came he escaped to the forest. In his wanderings he came upon a lion. His first instinct was to turn about and flee. Then he noticed that the lion seemed to be in great distress and was moaning and whimpering piteously.

As the slave came near, the lion put out his paw, which was swollen and bleeding. A large thorn had penetrated one of the lion's toes, and this was the cause of all of the animal's discomfort. Quickly Androcles pulled out the thorn and bound up the wounded paw. To show his gratitude the lion licked the man's hand like a dog, and then he led him to his cave for a shelter. Every day, after his wound had healed, he would go hunting in the forest and return with fresh meat for his master's refreshment.

But one day, when Androcles and the lion went out together, they were both captured and taken to the city to be used in the circus. The slave was to be thrown to the lion, after the animal had been kept

34

without food for several days to make him more ferocious.

The Emperor and all his court came to the arena to view the spectacle. The despairing slave was unchained and led out into the amphitheater before the Emperor's box. Then the lion was let loose, and rushed bounding and roaring toward his victim. But as soon as he came near Androcles he recognized his friend. To the surprise of the audience, the lion seemed to fawn upon the slave whom they had expected to see torn to shreds by the savage beast. Pleased by this unusual spectacle the Emperor summoned Androcles to him, and the slave told him the whole story. Thereupon the slave was pardoned and freed, and the lion set loose to return to his native forest.

ᘗ *Application*: GRATITUDE IS A QUALITY NOT LIM-
ITED TO MAN.

THE ANT AND
THE DOVE

A THIRSTY ANT went to a spring for a drink of water. While climbing down a blade of grass to reach the spring he fell in. The ant might very well have drowned had it not been for a dove who happened to be perched in a near-by tree. Seeing the ant's danger the dove quickly plucked off a leaf and let it drop into the water near the struggling insect. The ant climbed upon the leaf and presently was wafted safely ashore.

Just at that time a hunter was spreading his net in the hope of snaring the dove. The gratified ant, perceiving the hunter's plan, bit him in the heel. Startled, the huntsman dropped his net, and the dove flew away to safety.

ঙ্গ *Application*: ONE GOOD TURN DESERVES ANOTHER.

THE ONE-EYED
DOE

∾ A DOE who had had the misfortune to lose the sight of one of her eyes, and so could not see any-one approaching on that side, made it her practice to graze on a high cliff near the sea. Thus she kept her good eye toward the land on the lookout for hunters, while her blind side was toward the sea whence she feared no danger.

But one day some sailors were rowing past in a boat. Catching sight of the doe as she was grazing peacefully along the edge of the cliff, one of the sailors drew his bow and shot her. With her last gasp the dying doe said: "Alas, ill-fated creature that I am! I was safe on the land side, whence I looked for danger, but my enemy came from the sea, to which I looked for protection."

∾ *Application*: TROUBLE COMES FROM THE DIREC-
TION WE LEAST EXPECT IT.

THE ASS AND
HIS MASTERS

A DISCONTENTED ASS who felt that the gardener for whom he worked was a hard taskmaster appealed to Jupiter to give him another master. Annoyed by the ass's ingratitude, Jupiter bound him over to a potter who gave him even heavier burdens to bear.

Again the ass besought Jupiter. This time it was arranged to have him sold to a tanner. Finding that he had fallen into worse hands than ever, the ass said with a groan: "Alas, wretch that I am. Would that I had remained content with my former masters. My new owner not only works me harder while I am alive, but will not even spare my hide when I am dead!"

&ᴥ *Application*: HE THAT FINDS DISCONTENTMENT IN ONE PLACE IS NOT LIKELY TO FIND HAPPINESS IN ANOTHER.

THE LION AND THE
DOLPHIN

THE KING OF BEASTS was pacing majesti-cally along the shore of the sea one day when he spied a dolphin basking on the surface of the water.

"Hello, there, friend dolphin!" roared the lion. "This is a fortunate meeting, indeed. I long have wanted to suggest that you and I form an alliance. As I am the king of the beasts and you are the king of the fishes, what is more natural than that we should be strong friends and powerful allies?"

"There is much in what you say," replied the dolphin.

Not long afterward the lion again came to the sea-shore where he was challenged by a wild bull. The fight was not going too well for the lion, so he called upon the dolphin for his promised support. The latter, though ready and willing to aid his ally, found himself unable to come out of the sea to join the battle. After the wild bull had been put to flight, the lion upbraided the dolphin.

"You are a fine ally," said the lion. "I could have

been killed, and you never turned a fin to help me."

"Do not blame me," said the dolphin in reply, "but blame nature, which made me powerful in the sea but altogether helpless on land."

ᘒ *Application*: IN CHOOSING ALLIES LOOK TO THEIR POWER AS WELL AS THEIR WILL TO HELP YOU.

THE ASS'S
SHADOW

O N A HOT summer day a youth hired an ass to carry him from Athens to Megara. At mid-day the heat of the sun was so scorching that, feeling faint, he dismounted to rest himself in the shadow of the ass. Thereupon the driver disputed the place with him, declaring that he had an equal right to it with the other.

"What!" exclaimed the youth. "Did I not hire the ass for the whole journey?"

"Yes, indeed," said the driver, "you hired the ass, but you did not hire the ass's shadow."

And while they were wrangling the ass took to his heels and ran away.

Application: TOO MANY DISAGREEMENTS HAVE
NAUGHT BUT A SHADOW FOR A BASIS.

THE ASS EATING
THISTLES

𝕰 IT WAS HARVESTTIME and the master and the reapers were out in the field. When the sun was high in the sky the maidservants loaded the ass with good things to eat and drink and sent him to the field.

42

On his way he noticed a fine large thistle growing in the lane, and being hungry he began to eat it. As he chewed it slowly, he reflected: "How many greedy people would think themselves happy amidst such a variety of delicacies as I am carrying. But for my taste, this bitter, prickly thistle is more savory and appetizing than the most sumptuous banquet."

𝓏❧ *Application*: ONE MAN'S MEAT MAY BE ANOTHER MAN'S POISON.

43

THE HAWK AND
THE PIGEONS

A HAWK long had had his eye on a flock of pigeons, but no matter how often he had swooped down upon them from the sky they always had been able to reach their cote in safety. Thinking that it might be his shadow they had spied, he waited for a cloudy day for his next attack, but still to no avail.

At length the hungry hawk decided to use craft instead of attack. From the top of a near-by dead tree he called down to the pigeons: "Why do you prefer this life of constant fear and anxiety when, if you would make me your king, I could patrol the sky and make you safe from any attack that could be made upon you?"

The foolish pigeons, believing the hawk's interest in their welfare to be sincere, called him to the throne

44

as their king and protector. But no sooner was he established there than he issued an order that every day one pigeon would have to be sacrificed for his dinner.

ϑ➤ *Application*: THEY WHO VOLUNTARILY PUT THEM-
SELVES UNDER THE POWER OF A TY-
RANT DESERVE WHATEVER FATE
THEY RECEIVE.

45

THE BELLY AND THE
OTHER MEMBERS

∾ IT IS SAID that in former times the various members of the human body did not work together as amicably as they do now. On one occasion the members began to be critical of the belly for spending an idle life of luxury while they had to spend all their time laboring for its support and ministering to its wants and pleasures.

The members went so far as to decide to cut off the belly's supplies for the future. The hands were no longer to carry food to the mouth, nor the mouth to receive, nor the teeth to chew it.

But, lo and behold, it was only a short time after they had agreed upon this course of starving the belly into subjection when they all began, one by one, to fail and flop and the whole body to waste away. In the end the members became convinced that the belly also, cumbersome and useless as it seemed, had an important function of its own, and that they could no more exist without it than it could do without them.

∾ *Application*: AS IN THE BODY, SO IN THE STATE, EACH MEMBER IN HIS PROPER SPHERE MUST WORK FOR THE COMMON GOOD.

46

THE FROGS DESIRING
A KING

THE FROGS always had lived a happy life in the marshes. They had jumped and splashed about with never a care in the world. Yet some of them were not satisfied with their easygoing life. They thought they should have a king to rule over them and to watch over their morals. So they decided to send a petition to Jupiter asking him to appoint a king.

Jupiter was amused by the frogs' plea. Good-naturedly he threw down a log into the lake, which landed with such a splash that it sent all the frogs scampering for safety. But after a while, when one venturesome frog saw that the log lay still, he encouraged his friends to approach the fallen monster. In no time at all the frogs, growing bolder and bolder, swarmed over the log Jupiter had sent and treated it with the greatest contempt.

47

Dissatisfied with so tame a ruler, they petitioned Jupiter a second time, saying: "We want a real king, a king who will really rule over us." Jupiter, by this time, had lost some of his good nature and was tired of the frogs' complaining.

So he sent them a stork, who proceeded to gobble up the frogs right and left. After a few days the survivors sent Mercury with a private message to Jupiter, beseeching him to take pity on them once more.

"Tell them," said Jupiter coldly, "that this is their own doing. They wanted a king. Now they will have to make the best of what they asked for."

ᘛ *Application*: LET WELL ENOUGH ALONE!

THE HEN AND
THE FOX

A FOX was out looking for a late supper. He came to a henhouse, and through the open door he could see a hen far up on the highest perch, safe out of his reach.

Here, thought the fox, was a case for diplomacy. Either that or go hungry! So he gave considerable thought to just how he should approach his intended supper.

"Hello, there, friend hen," said he in an anxious voice. "I haven't seen you about of late. Somebody told me that you have had a sick spell and I was sincerely worried over you. You look pale as a ghost. If you will just step down I'll take your pulse and look at your tongue. I'm afraid you are in for quite a siege."

49

"You never said a truer word, cousin fox," replied the hen. "It will have to be a siege, for I am in such a state that if I were to climb down to where you are, I'm afraid it would be the death of me."

𝓫 *Application:* BEWARE OF THE INSINCERE FRIEND!

THE CAT AND
THE MICE

&~ A CAT, GROWN FEEBLE with age, and no longer able to hunt for mice as she was wont to do, sat in the sun and bethought herself how she might entice them within reach of her paws.

The idea came to her that if she would suspend herself by the hind legs from a peg in the closet wall, the mice, believing her to be dead, no longer would be afraid of her. So, at great pains and with the assistance of a torn pillow case she was able to carry out her plan.

But before the mice could approach within range of the innocent-looking paws a wise old gaffer-mouse whispered to his friends: "Keep your distance, my friends. Many a bag have I seen in my day, but never one with a cat's head at the bottom of it."

Then turning to the uncomfortable feline, he said: "Hang there, good madam, as long as you please, but I would not trust myself within reach of you though you were stuffed with straw."

&~ *Application*: HE WHO IS ONCE DECEIVED IS DOU-
BLY CAUTIOUS.

51

THE MILLER, HIS SON,
AND THEIR DONKEY

A MILLER AND HIS SON were driving their donkey to a neighboring fair to sell him. They had not gone far when they met a group of girls returning from town laughing and talking together.

"Look there!" cried one of them. "Did you ever see such fools, to be trudging along the road on foot, when they ought to be riding!"

So the man put the boy on the donkey, and they went on their way. Presently they came up to a group of old men in earnest debate. "There!" said one of them. "That proves exactly what I was saying. No one pays any respect to old age in these days. Look at that idle young rogue riding, while his poor old father has to walk. Get down, you lazy lout, and let the old man rest his weary limbs."

The miller made his son dismount, and got on the donkey's back in his place. And in this manner they

proceeded along the way until they met a company
of women and children.

"Why, shame on you, lazybones!" they cried.
"How can you ride while that poor little lad can
hardly keep up with you?" The good miller, wishing
to please, took up his son to sit behind him.

But just as they reached the edge of the village a
townsman called out to them: "I have a good mind
to report you to the authorities for overloading that
poor beast so shamelessly. You big hulking fellows
should better be able to carry that donkey than the
other way round."

So, alighting, the miller and his son tied the beast's legs together, and with a pole across their shoulders, carried the donkey over the bridge that led to the town. This was such an entertaining sight to the townsfolk that crowds came out to laugh at it. The poor animal, frightened by the uproar, began to struggle to free himself. In the midst of the turmoil the ass slipped off the pole and over the rail of the bridge into the water and was drowned.

&❧ *Application*: TRY TO PLEASE ALL AND YOU END BY PLEASING NONE.

THE ASS, THE COCK,
AND THE LION

AN ASS AND A COCK lived at peace in a farmyard together. But one day a hungry lion chanced to pass that way. Seeing the ass so plump and well fed, he resolved to make a meal of him.

Now, they say that there is nothing that annoys a lion so much as to hear a cock crow. At that very moment the cock gave one of his proudest cock-a-doodle-doos, causing the lion to make off with all haste from the spot.

The ass, greatly amused to see the mighty lion routed by the mere crowing of a barnyard fowl, boldly galloped after the retreating king of beasts. He had, however, pursued him only a short distance, when the lion turned sharply upon the foolish ass, and with a mighty roar leaped upon him and made an end of him.

&❧ *Application*: FALSE CONFIDENCE IS THE FORE-RUNNER OF MISFORTUNE.

THE LION AND
THE GOAT

ONE VERY HOT summer day, when the ground was dry and many streams were dry, a lion and a goat came at the same time to quench their thirst at the same small mountain spring.

As they looked up and saw each other they at once fell to quarreling over which was to drink first of the water. They even forgot their great thirst, so determined was each that he was to have the first drink. Just as they were about ready to fly at each other they chanced to look up. There, circling about in the blue sky over their heads they saw a flock of vultures, hovering and waiting to pounce upon whichever should fall in defeat.

Grinning foolishly at each other, the lion and the goat said in almost the same breath: "I insist, dear friend, that *you* shall take the first drink at the spring!"

Application: IT IS BETTER TO DRINK SECOND AT THE SPRING THAN TO FURNISH FOOD FOR THE VULTURES.

56

THE FOX AND
THE LION

O NE DAY a fox who had never seen a lion was walking in the wood. Suddenly the king of beasts stood in the path before him, and the fox almost died of fright. He ran away and hid himself in his den. The next time he came upon the lion he merely paused to allow the majestic beast to pass by. The third time they met the fox boldly approached the lion and passed the time of day with him and asked after his family's health.

֍ *Application*: FAMILIARITY BREEDS CONTEMPT.

THE CROW AND
THE PITCHER

〰 A CROW, so thirsty that he could not even caw, came upon a pitcher which once had been full of water. But when he put his beak into the pitcher's mouth he found that only a little water was left in it. Strain and strive as he might he was not able to reach far enough down to get at it. He tried to break the pitcher, then to overturn it, but his strength was not equal to the task.

Just as he was about to give up in despair a thought came to him. He picked up a pebble and dropped it into the pitcher. Then he took another pebble and dropped that into the pitcher. One by one he kept dropping pebbles into the pitcher until the water mounted to the brim. Then perching himself upon the handle he drank and drank until his thirst was quenched.

ॐ *Application*: NECESSITY IS THE MOTHER OF IN-VENTION.

THE BOASTING
TRAVELER

A YOUNG MAN who had been traveling in foreign parts returned to his
home city where he bragged and boasted to all who
would listen of the great feats he had accomplished
in the places he had visited.

"Why, when I was in Rhodes," he shouted, thump-
ing his chest, "I made the most extraordinary leap
the people of that place ever had seen. I have witnesses to prove it, too."

In time his hearers became weary of the traveler's
boasts, and one of them said: "These exploits of
yours in Rhodes may all be true, but you can save
yourself much breath by doing one of those marvel-
ous leaps right now instead of merely talking about
it."

* *Application*: HE WHO DOES A THING WELL DOES
NOT NEED TO BOAST.

THE EAGLE, THE
WILDCAT, AND THE SOW

ટ્ AN EAGLE chose the top branches of an old oak tree for her nest and hatched her young there. A wildcat had selected the hollow trunk of the same tree for her den where she would raise her little ones. And down among the roots of the old oak a sow had burrowed a hole where she planned to raise her piglets in comfort.

For some time all three families lived peaceably in the old oak, until the wildcat took the notion to start gossiping about her neighbors.

"Neighbor," she whispered to the eagle, "as you know I have the highest respect for that old sow down below. But if she keeps rooting under this tree the whole thing will come crashing down someday. That's probably what she has in mind so she can feed our babies to her litter."

Needless to say, the mother eagle was worried. She was so disturbed that she did not dare to leave her nest to go in search of food. Meanwhile, the gossiping wildcat visited the sow.

"Mrs. Sow," she whispered, "I'm no gossip, as you know, but if I were you I wouldn't leave home today.

I overheard that eagle upstairs telling her children they were going to have pork for supper."

So the eagle stayed in her nest and the sow remained with her little pigs. But the wildcat sneaked off every night and got all the food for her kittens, while her neighbors lived in distrust of each other.

It is possible that both families would have starved to death had not the wildcat made the mistake of getting caught in a hunter's snare, and the sow and the eagle became reunited in caring for the abandoned kittens.

ઙ *Application*: GOSSIPS ARE TO BE SEEN AND NOT HEARD.

THE ASS AND THE
GRASSHOPPER

ONE FINE SUMMER DAY an ass heard some grasshoppers chirping and singing merrily. Delighted with the music, and hoping to learn the secret of their musical ability, the ass approached them.

"My fine fellows," said he, "upon what do you feed that makes you sing so sweetly all day long?"

When the grasshoppers told the foolish ass that they supped upon nothing but dew, he galloped off determined to exist upon the same diet. In due time he died of hunger.

Application: EVEN A FOOL IS WISE—WHEN IT IS TOO LATE!

THE HEIFER AND
THE OX

ઠ્ક THERE WAS ONCE a young heifer who, never having felt the yoke, gamboled about in the fields as free as the wind. With her tail in the air she frisked up to the old ox who was pulling a plow for the farmer.

"How foolish you are," she said to the toiling ox, "to work so hard all day long. Why don't you do as I do, enjoy life, go and come as you will, instead of submitting to such drudgery day in, day out?"

The old ox said nothing, but went on with his work. When evening came he was turned loose by the farmer, and he went over to the village altar where the priests were preparing to offer the heifer as a sacrifice.

The ox approached the heifer and said: "How do you feel about it now? You must know now why you were allowed to live in idleness. As for me, I had rather my neck felt the weight of the yoke than of the knife."

ઠ્ક *Application*: HE LAUGHS BEST WHO LAUGHS LAST.

THE FOX AND
THE STORK

რ ONE DAY a fox invited a stork to have dinner with him, and the stork accepted. The fox, who enjoyed some reputation as a practical joker, provided nothing for dinner but some thin soup in a shallow dish. This the fox lapped up very readily, while the stork, unable to gain a mouthful with her long bill, was as hungry at the end of the dinner as when she began.

As they were parting the fox professed his regret that his guest had eaten so sparingly, and feared that the dish was not seasoned to her satisfaction. The stork replied: "Please do not apologize, friend fox, I have had a most interesting evening. Will you not do me the honor one week hence to return the visit and dine with me?"

True to his appointment the fox arrived, and the stork ordered the dinner to be brought in. But when it was served up, the fox found to his dismay that it

was contained in a very long-necked jar with a narrow mouth. The stork readily thrust her long bill into the jar and enjoyed her dinner, while the fox was obliged to content himself with licking the neck of the jar. As the fox made his adieus with as good grace as he could muster, the stork said dryly: "I hope you do not expect an apology for the dinner."

ঙ *Application*: MANY GO OUT FOR WOOL AND COME HOME SHORN.

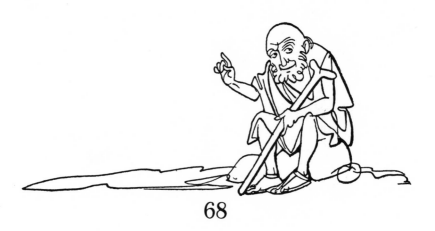

68

THE FARMER AND THE
NIGHTINGALE

AFTER a hard day's work a farmer went early to bed. But he could not go to sleep because of the melodious singing of a nightingale all through the summer night. So pleased was he by the bird's song that the next night he set a trap for it and captured it.

"Ah, my beauty," said he, "now that I have caught you, you shall hang in a cage and sing for me every night."

"But we nightingales never sing in a cage," replied the bird. "If you imprison me I shall sicken and die and you shall never hear my song again."

"Then I'll put you in a pie and eat you," said the farmer. "I always have heard that nightingale pie is a dainty morsel."

"Please do not kill me," begged the nightingale. "If you will set me free I'll tell you three great truths

69

that will be worth far more to you than my poor body."

So the farmer set him loose, and he flew up to a branch of a tree.

"Hold on," said the farmer, "what are the three great truths you promised me?"

The nightingale trilled a few happy notes and said: "Never believe a captive's promise. Keep what you have. And never sorrow over what is lost forever." Then the songbird flew away.

ঌ *Application*: A BIRD IN THE CAGE IS WORTH TWO ON A BRANCH.

THE ASS AND
THE LAP DOG

AN ASS AND A LAP DOG belonged to the same master. Tied up in the stable the ass had plenty of corn and hay to eat, and he should have been more than contented with his lot, even though he was kept busy hauling wood all day, and on occasion had to take his turn at the mill at night.

Meanwhile the little dog was always sporting and gamboling about, caressing and fawning upon his master to such an extent that he became a great favorite, and was permitted to lie in his master's lap. Needless to say, the ass began to feel sorry for himself. It galled him to see the lap dog living in such ease and luxury, enjoying the favor of the master.

Thinking that if he behaved in the same fashion toward his master he would fare the same, one day he broke from his halter and rushed into the house where his owner was at meat. Here he pranced about, swishing his tail and imitating as best he

71

could the frolics of the lap dog, finally upsetting the dinner table and smashing all the crockery. Nor did

he stop there. He jumped upon his master and pawed him with his roughshod feet.

At length the servants, seeing their master in no little danger, released him from the ass's wild caresses. Thereupon they so belabored the silly creature with sticks and stones that he never got up again.

&bw; *Application*: TO BE SATISFIED WITH ONE'S LOT IS BETTER THAN TO DESIRE SOMETHING WHICH ONE IS NOT FITTED TO RECEIVE.

THE COCK AND
THE JEWEL

ONE BRIGHT DAY in the spring a cock was scratching up the straw that littered the barnyard in search of food for his flock of hens. To his great surprise, his industrious claws turned up a jewel that by some chance had been lost there.

Now, the cock was a sensible cock. "Ho," said he, as his bright eyes examined the jewel, "I can see you are a very valuable thing, though how you got here I have not the least idea. I can see, too, that there are those who must prize you, but as for me, give me a kernel of corn rather than all the bright jewels in the world."

Application: THE IGNORANT DESPISE WHAT IS PRECIOUS ONLY BECAUSE THEY CANNOT UNDERSTAND IT.

JUPITER AND THE BEE

LONG, LONG AGO there was an industrious bee who had stored her combs with a bountiful harvest. One day she decided to fly up to heaven to present an offering of honey to Jupiter. The god was so delighted with the bee's gift that he promised her she should have whatever her heart desired.

"Oh, great Jupiter, my creator and my master, I beg of thee, give thy servant a sting, so that when anyone approaches my hive to take the honey, I may kill him on the spot."

Jupiter was surprised to hear such a bloodthirsty request from such a humble creature. Becoming angry, he said: "Your prayer shall not be granted in exactly the way you wish. But the sting you ask for you shall have. When anyone comes to take away your honey and you attack him, the wound shall be fatal. But it shall be fatal *to you*, for your life shall go with your sting."

Application: HE WHO PRAYS HARD AGAINST HIS NEIGHBOR BRINGS A CURSE UPON HIMSELF.

74

THE HORSE AND
THE GROOM

&ea; ONCE THERE WAS a groom who was just about the meanest man in the world. He used to steal the grain intended for the horse and, without his master's knowledge, sell it in the village. But all day long he kept very busy grooming and currying the horse within an inch of its life.

"If you really are so anxious that I look well," said the horse one day to his groom, "then give me less of your brushing and more of your corn."

ço *Application*: A MAN MAY SMILE, YET BE A VILLAIN.

76

THE MISCHIEVOUS
DOG

&~ ONCE UPON A TIME there was a dog who was so wild and mischievous that his master despaired of taming him. The last straw was when he bit a servant in pretending to be playful. His master was taking him out to the forest to dispose of him when a neighbor suggested: "The way to tame that beast is to fasten a chain around his neck and attach a heavy wooden clog to the end of it. That will stop him from biting and worrying his fellows."

The master decided to try it. The next day the dog, looking upon his clog as a badge of distinction, went down to the market place, shaking and rattling the hobble to attract everyone's attention. An old dog approached him and said: "If I were in your place I would make less noise and not call people's attention to my disgrace. Wearing a hobble is anything but a mark of distinction!"

&~ *Application*: MEN OFTEN MISTAKE NOTORIETY
FOR FAME.

THE BLIND MAN AND
THE WHELP

THERE WAS ONCE a blind man who, merely by placing his hands upon an animal, could determine to what species it belonged. To test him one day they brought him a wolf's whelp. Long and carefully he felt the beast all over. Then, still being in doubt, he said: "I know not whether thy father was a dog or a wolf, but this I do know, that I would not trust thee among a flock of sheep."

ɞ *Application*: THE CHILD IS FATHER TO THE MAN.

THE HARES AND
THE FROGS

&ᴖ FOR A LONG TIME the hares had believed themselves the most persecuted of all the animals. Everyone was their enemy, they said. One day, when the
prospect looked especially dark, they came to the
sad resolution that there was nothing left for them
but to make away with themselves, one and all. So
off they ran to a lake near by, determined to throw
themselves into the water to be drowned.

But at their approach a school of frogs seated on
the shore took fright and dived into the water.

"Hold up!" cried the hare who was in the lead.
"Let us not be too hasty. Surely our case is not so
desperate yet, for here are other poor creatures even
more fainthearted than ourselves."

&ᴖ *Application*: THERE IS ALWAYS SOMEONE WORSE
OFF THAN YOURSELF.

THE COCK AND THE FOX

A FOX was trotting past a farmyard early one morning when he heard a cock crowing. Upon investigation he found that chanticleer was perched in a tall tree far out of reach of anyone who might be entertaining thoughts of having him for breakfast.

"Why, cousin cock," the fox called up to the bird in the tall tree, "what a pleasure it is to see you! Won't you come down and let me greet you properly?"

"I would love to," replied the cock (who was no fool), "but, as you know, there are some animals who would like nothing better than to grab me and eat me."

"Why, my dear cousin," exclaimed the fox, "do you mean to say you haven't heard the news? All the animals have agreed to live in peace with one another."

80

While the fox was speaking, the cock kept craning his neck as though he could see something very interesting in the distance. Naturally, the fox was consumed with curiosity.

"Cousin, what in the world do you see up there that is so interesting?"

"Oh, nothing much—just a pack of hounds headed in this direction and coming at a fast clip," said the cock.

"Please excuse me," said the fox nervously. "I just thought of something I had forgotten."

"What's the hurry?" asked the cock. "I was just coming down for a talk. You don't mean to say that you have anything to be afraid of now that you know about the wonderful peace plan?"

"Well," replied the fox, as he started to run, "maybe those hounds haven't heard about it yet!"

ॐ *Application*: THE BEST LIARS OFTEN GET CAUGHT IN THEIR OWN LIES.

THE EAGLE AND
THE FOX

AN EAGLE AND A FOX long had lived together as good neighbors, the eagle at the top of a high tree and the fox in a hole at the foot of it. One day, however, while the fox was away, the eagle, seeking a tender morsel for her nestful of young ones, swooped down upon the fox's cub and carried it away to her nest.

The fox, on her return home, upbraided the eagle for this breach of friendship, and pleaded with the eagle to return the cub to her den. But the eagle, feeling sure that her own brood high up in their treetop nest were safe from any possible revenge, ignored the entreaties of the cub's mother.

Quickly running to the place where she knew an altar fire to be burning, the fox snatched a brand and hurried back to the tree. The mother eagle, who was

just on the point of tearing the cub to pieces to feed to her babies, looked down and saw that the fox was going to set fire to the tree and burn it and her nest and eaglets to ashes.

"Hold on, dear neighbor!" she screamed. "Don't set fire to our tree. I'll bring back your cub to you safe and sound!"

☙ *Application*: DO UNTO OTHERS AS YOU WOULD HAVE THEM DO UNTO YOU.

THE HORSE AND
THE LADEN ASS

ONCE THERE WAS a man who kept a horse and an ass as beasts of burden. It was his custom to load the ass until he could barely stagger under the weight, while the horse was allowed to prance along in its fine trappings with a very light load.

As they were proceeding along the road one day, the ass, who had been ailing for the past several days, said to the horse: "Will you relieve me of part of my load for a few miles? I feel dreadfully unwell, but if you will carry a fair portion of the freight today I shall soon get well again. This weight is killing me."

The horse, however, merely kicked up his heels and told the ass not to trouble him with his complaints. The ass staggered along for another half mile in silence, then suddenly fell to the ground dead.

Just then the master came up, and perceiving what had happened, he removed the load from the

dead ass and placed it on the horse's back. "Alas,"
groaned the horse, as he started off with the heavy
load augmented by the carcass of the dead ass, "now
am I rewarded for my ill-nature. By refusing to bear
my fair share of the load, I now must carry the whole
of it plus the dead weight of my poor companion."

Application: A BAD TEMPER CARRIES WITH IT ITS
OWN PUNISHMENT.

THE MISER

છ A MISER, who never stopped worrying about the safety of his many possessions, sold all his property and converted it into a huge lump of gold. This he buried in a hole in the ground near his garden wall, and every morning he went to visit it and gloat over the size of it.

The miser's strange behavior aroused the curiosity of the town thief. Spying upon the rich man from some bushes, the thief saw him place the lump of gold back in the hole and cover it up. As soon as the miser's back was turned, the thief went to the spot, dug up the gold and took it away.

The next morning when the miser came to gloat over his treasure he found nothing but an empty hole. He wept and tore his hair, and so loud were his lamentations that a neighbor came running to see what was the trouble. As soon as he had learned the cause of it, he said comfortingly: "You are foolish to distress yourself so over something that was buried in the earth. Take a stone and put it in the hole, and think that it is your lump of gold. You never meant to use it anyway. Therefore it will do you just as much good to fondle a lump of granite as a lump of gold."

ॐ *Application*: THE TRUE VALUE OF MONEY IS NOT IN ITS POSSESSION BUT IN ITS USE.

THE KID AND
THE WOLF

T HERE WAS ONCE a very active kid who would leave the other goats in the farmyard below and climb onto the steep roof of the farmhouse.

"Look at me, mother," he would call down. "You are afraid to come up here where I am." The other goats paid very little attention to the boasting kid, but one day a wolf passed by the farmhouse. He gave one look at the kid on the rooftree and would have passed by since it was easy to see that here was one dinner that was safe out of his reach. But the kid jeered and bleated: "Why don't you try to come up and catch me, coward?"

The wolf stopped, looked up again, and called back: "It is not you who call me coward, but the place on which you are standing."

&❧ *Application*: IF YOU MUST REVILE YOUR NEIGH-
BOR, MAKE CERTAIN FIRST THAT HE
CANNOT REACH YOU.

THE PORCUPINE
AND THE SNAKES

&bl; A PORCUPINE had selected a comfortable cave for his home only to find it already occupied by a family of snakes.

"Would it be agreeable if I used one corner of your cave to spend the winter?" he asked. The snakes very generously offered to share their home with the porcupine, and he moved in, curled up in a ball, stuck out all his prickly quills and settled down for the winter.

It was not long, however, before the snakes realized that they had made a mistake, for every time one of them moved he would prick himself on one of the visitor's quills.

After bearing this discomfort for a time the snakes got up their courage to complain to the porcupine.

"That's just too bad," said their guest. "I am most comfortable here. But if you snakes aren't satisfied, why don't you move out?" And he curled up once more and resumed his nap.

&bl; *Application*: IT IS SAFER TO KNOW ONE'S GUEST BEFORE OFFERING HOSPITALITY.

THE FALCONER AND
THE PARTRIDGE

A FALCONER discovered that he had captured a partridge in his net. The bird cried out piteously when he approached: "Please, Master Falconer, let me go. If you will set me free I promise you that I will decoy other partridges into your net."

"No," replied the falconer. "I might have set you free. But one who is ready to betray his innocent friends to save his own miserable life deserves, if possible, worse than death."

Application: TREACHERY IS THE BASEST CRIME OF ALL.

THE CREAKING WHEELS

ࢌ SLOWLY and ponderously over the dusty road a yoke of oxen were hauling a heavily laden wagon. Each time the wheels turned on their axles they set up a tremendous creaking. Driven almost frantic by the ear-piercing noise, the driver cried: "Wagon, why do you make all this clamor and complaint, when they who are drawing all the weight are silent?"

ࢌ *Application*: HE WHO GROANS LOUDEST IS OFTEN THE LEAST HURT.

JUPITER, NEPTUNE, MINERVA, AND MOMUS

ଛିକ IN ANCIENT TIMES, when the world was young, Jupiter, Neptune, and Minerva used to spend a great deal of time disputing as to which could make the most perfect thing. So it was decided that they would have a contest with Momus (at that time he had not yet been turned out of Olympus) to decide which creation had the greatest merit.

Jupiter made a man. Neptune made a bull. Minerva made a house. Then Judge Momus came to judge the contest. He began by finding fault with Neptune's bull because his horns were not below his eyes so that he could see when he gored with them. Next he found fault with the man because there was no window in his breast in order that all might see his inward thoughts and feelings. And lastly he found fault with the house because it had no wheels to enable its inhabitants to move away from bad neighbors.

Jupiter, incensed with the carping critic who could not be pleased, forthwith drove the fault-finding judge out of the home of the gods.

ॐ *Application*: IT IS TIME TO CRITICIZE THE WORKS OF OTHERS WHEN YOU HAVE DONE SOME GOOD THING YOURSELF.

THE LION IN
LOVE

IT HAPPENED in days of old that a lion fell in love with the beautiful daughter of a woodman, and one day he came to ask the maiden's hand in marriage. It was only natural that the woodman was not greatly pleased with the lion's offer, and he declined the honor of so dangerous an alliance.

Then the lion threatened the parents of the maiden with his royal displeasure. The poor father did not know what to do. Finally he said: "We are greatly flattered by your proposal. But, you see, our daughter is a tender child, and her mother and I fear that in expressing your affection for her you may do her an injury. Would your majesty consent to having your claws removed and your teeth extracted before becoming a bridegroom?"

So deeply was the lion in love that he permitted

the operation to take place. But when he came again
to the woodman's home to claim the maiden for his
bride the father, no longer afraid of the tamed and
disarmed king of beasts, seized a stout club and drove
the unhappy suitor from his door.

ဝ Application: EVEN THE WILDEST CAN BE TAMED
BY LOVE.

THE FOX WITHOUT
A TAIL

A FOX had the misfortune to have his bushy tail caught in a trap. When he saw that it was a question of his life or his tail he left his tail behind him. He felt himself disgraced, however, and for a time did not go near his friends for fear of ridicule.

But one day the idea came to him how he could make the best of a bad bargain. He called a meeting of all the rest of the foxes and proposed to them that they should follow his example.

"You have no idea," said he, "of the ease and comfort I am enjoying. I don't know why I didn't cut off my tail long ago. I could never have believed it if I had not tried it myself. When you come to think about it, friends, a tail is such an inconvenient and unnecessary appendage that it is strange we have

96

put up with it so long. My sincere advice to you all is to share this new freedom and part with your tails at once."

As he concluded, one of the older and wiser foxes stepped forward and said: "There is not one of us who does not believe that you found it convenient to cut off your tail. However, we are not so convinced that you would advise us to part with our tails if there were any chance of recovering your own."

ʚ❧ *Application*: MISERY LOVES COMPANY.

THE ARAB AND
THE CAMEL

THE ARAB tugged and pulled as he tightened the ropes which held the heavy bales and boxes to the kneeling camel's back. Then, as the camel arose, his master said jokingly: "What is your preference, camel, the road that goes up hill or the road that goes down?"

"Pray, master," said the camel dryly, "since you leave the choice to me, I would prefer the road that runs along the level plain."

Application: A LEVEL PATH IS PLEASING TO THE LADEN BEAST.

98

THE RAVEN AND
THE SWAN

THE RAVEN, who earned a comfortable live-lihood picking up scraps, became dissatisfied with his lot. He would be especially unhappy whenever he saw the swan floating gracefully about a near-by pool.

"What makes that swan so white and beautiful?" he would say. "Could it be that the water has magic qualities to turn one's feathers from black to white?"

So the raven left his comfortable home and betook himself to the pools and streams. There he washed and plumed his feathers, but all to no purpose. His plumage remained as black as ever, and before long he perished for want of his usual food.

ॐ *Application*: A CHANGE OF SCENE DOES NOT
CHANGE ONE'S CHARACTER.

HERCULES AND THE WAGONER

A LAZY FARM HAND was carelessly driving his wagon along a muddy road, when the wheels became stuck so fast in the clay that the horses could no longer pull the load.

The wagoner got down, and without making the least effort toward extricating the cart from the mire, he began to pray for Hercules, the god of strength, to come and help him out of his trouble.

But Hercules, annoyed by the man's helplessness, called down from above: "Get up from your knees, lazybones, and put your shoulder to the wheel."

Application: THE GODS HELP THEM THAT HELP THEMSELVES.

THE MAN AND
THE SATYR

౼ A MAN AND A SATYR met on a woodland path, and as they journeyed along they struck up an acquaintance. The day was wintery and cold, and while they sat resting on a log the man put his fingers to his mouth and blew on them.

"What's that for, my friend?" asked the satyr.

"Oh, I always do that," replied the man, "when my hands are cold. I blow on them to warm them."

Shortly afterward they arrived at the satyr's home, and he invited his companion in for a bowl of hot porridge. As the host placed a steaming bowl before his guest, the man raised his spoon to his lips and began blowing on it.

"And now what are you doing?" asked the satyr.

"Oh, my porridge is too hot to swallow, so I am blowing on it to cool it off," replied the man. And he went on blowing while the satyr stared in amazement.

Application: SOME MEN CAN BLOW HOT AND BLOW COLD WITH THE SAME BREATH.

THE LARK AND HER
YOUNG ONES

A LARK, who had her nest of young ones in a wheat field, had to leave them each day to go out and hunt food for them. As the wheat ripened, the mother, expecting the arrival of the reapers, left word that the young larks should report to her all the news they heard.

One day, while she was absent, the farmer came to view his crop. "It is high time," he called to his son, "that our grain is cut. Go, tell all our neighbors to come early in the morning to help us reap it." When the mother lark came her children told her what they had heard, and begged her to remove them to a place of safety. "There's plenty of time," said she. "If friend farmer waits for his neighbors to help him, there's no danger of the grain being harvested tomorrow."

103

The next day, the owner came again, and finding the day warmer and the wheat dead-ripe and nothing done, said to his son: "There is not a moment to be lost. We cannot depend upon our neighbors, we must call in all of our relatives. You run now and call all your uncles and cousins and tell them to be here bright and early tomorrow morning to begin the harvest."

In still greater fear, the young larks repeated to their mother the farmer's words when she came home to her nest. "If that is all," she said, "then do not let it frighten you, for relatives always have harvesting of their own to do. But I want you to listen very carefully to what you hear the next time, and be sure to let me know what is said."

The next day while she was away the farmer came as before, and finding the grain almost ready to fall to the ground from overripeness, and still no one at work, called to his son: "We can't wait for our neighbors and relatives any longer. You and I are going to the barn right now and sharpen our sickles. At dawn tomorrow morning we shall get to work and harvest the grain ourselves."

When the young larks told their mother what they had heard the farmer say, she cried: "Then it is time to be off, indeed. If the master has made up his mind to undertake the work himself, then the grain really will be cut." So the mother lark moved her nest, and the next day the farmer and his son came with their sickles and harvested the wheat.

Application: IF YOU WANT A TASK WELL DONE, THEN DO IT YOURSELF.

THE BOY AND THE
FILBERTS

A BOY put his hand into a pitcher which contained a goodly quantity of figs and filberts. Greedily he clutched as many as his fist could possibly hold. But when he tried to pull it out, the narrowness of the neck of the vessel prevented him.

Unwilling to lose any of the nuts, yet unable to draw out his hand, the lad burst into tears, bitterly bewailing his hard fortune. An honest fellow standing near by gave him this wise and reasonable advice: "Grasp only half the quantity, my boy, and you will easily succeed."

Application: HALF A LOAF IS BETTER THAN NO BREAD.

106

THE LION, THE ASS, AND THE FOX

᠌᠌ A LION, an ass, and a fox formed a hunting party, and after an exciting chase caught and killed a great stag. All three were hungry, but the lion especially so. "Here, friend ass," he roared, "divide up the spoils, and let's have our dinner. I'm just about starved."

The ass was trying his best to divide the carcass into three equal portions when the lion fell upon him with a roar and tore him to pieces.

"Now," said the lion to the fox, "let's see how good you are at dividing the stag into two parts."

Taking one look at the remains of the poor ass, the fox said never a word, but made sure that in the division of the meat he left the "lion's share" for the king of beasts and only a mouthful for himself.

The lion nodded approvingly. "A very fair division, indeed," said he. "Who could have taught you to divide so fairly?"

"If I needed any lesson," replied the fox, "I had only to look at the body of our late friend, the ass, over yonder."

᠌᠌ *Application*: WE LEARN BY THE MISFORTUNES OF OTHERS.

THE FROG AND
THE OX

SOME LITTLE FROGS had just had a har-
rowing experience down at the swampy
meadow, and they came hopping home to report
their adventure.

"Oh, father," said one of the little frogs, all out of
breath, "we have just seen the most terrible monster
in all the world. It was enormous, with horns on its
head and a long tail and hoofs—"

"Why, child, that was no monster. That was only
an ox. He isn't so big! If I really put my mind to it I
could make myself as big as an ox. Just watch me!"
So the old frog blew himself up. "Was he as big as I
am now?" he asked.

"Oh, father, much bigger," cried the little frogs.
Again the father frog blew himself up, and asked his
children if the ox could be as big as that.

"Bigger, father, a great deal bigger" came the

chorus from the little frogs. "If you blew yourself up until you burst you could not be as big as the monster we saw in the swampy meadow."

Provoked by such disparagement of his powers, the old frog made one more attempt. He blew and blew and swelled and swelled until something went *pop*. The old frog had burst.

~ *Application*: SELF-CONCEIT LEADS TO SELF-DESTRUCTION

THE LION, THE BEAR,
AND THE FOX

A LION AND A BEAR found the carcass of a fawn. Both were hungry. Both wanted it. So they started to fight for it. The contest was long and hard and savage. At last, when both of them, half blinded and half dead, lay panting on the ground without the strength to touch the prize before them, a fox came by.

Noting the helpless condition of the two beasts, the impudent fox stepped nimbly between them, seized the fawn over which they had battled, and with never a "thank you" dragged it away to his den.

ᔬ *Application*: ONLY FOOLS FIGHT TO EXHAUSTION WHILE A ROGUE RUNS OFF WITH THE DINNER.

THE CAT AND
THE FOX

 A FOX was boasting to a cat one day about how clever he was. "Why, I have a whole bag of tricks,"

he bragged. "For instance, I know of at least a hundred different ways of escaping my enemies, the dogs."

"How remarkable," said the cat. "As for me, I have only one trick, though I usually make it work. I wish you could teach me some of yours."

"Well, sometime when I have nothing else to do," said the fox, "I might teach you one or two of my easier ones."

Just at that moment they heard the yelping of a pack of hounds. They were coming straight toward the spot where the cat and the fox stood. Like a flash the cat scampered up a tree and disappeared in the foliage. "This is the trick I told you about," she called down to the fox. "It's my only one. Which trick are you going to use?"

The fox sat there trying to decide which of his many tricks he was going to employ. Nearer and nearer came the hounds. When it was quite too late, the fox decided to run for it. But even before he started the dogs were upon him, and that was the end of the fox, bagful of tricks and all!

Application: ONE GOOD PLAN THAT WORKS IS BETTER THAN A HUNDRED DOUBTFUL ONES.

THE MONKEY AND
THE CAMEL

AT A GREAT GATHERING of all the beasts the monkey got up to entertain his friends by doing a dance. So nimble were his feet and so amusing his gestures and grimaces that all the animals roared with laughter. Even the lion, the king of beasts, forgot his royal dignity and rolled on the ground with glee.

Only the camel seemed to be bored by the monkey's performance. "I don't see anything so funny in that exhibition," she sniffed. "As a matter of fact, it seems very crude and amateurish to me."

"All right, then," cried all the animals, "suppose you show us what you can do!"

Realizing what she had let herself in for, the camel shambled into the circle, and in no time at all had made herself utterly ridiculous by her awkward and stumbling performance. All the beasts booed her and set upon her with clubs and claws and drove her out into the desert.

᠁ *Application*: STRETCH YOUR ARM NO FARTHER
THAN YOUR SLEEVE WILL REACH.

THE ASS IN THE
LION'S SKIN

ONCE UPON A TIME an ass found a lion's skin and put it on. In this disguise he roamed about, frightening all the silly animals he met. When a fox came along, the ass in the lion's skin tried to frighten him too. But the fox, having heard his voice, said: "If you really want to frighten me you will have to disguise your bray."

℘ *Application*: CLOTHES MAY DISGUISE A FOOL, BUT
HIS WORDS WILL GIVE HIM AWAY.

THE HAWK AND
THE FARMER

᠑᠍ A PRUDENT FARMER had spread a net over his cornfield to catch the crows who liked to dig up his newly planted seeds. One day a hawk, pursuing a pigeon, flew so swiftly over the farmer's cornfield that before he knew it he found himself caught in the snare.

The farmer, observing the hawk struggling in the net, went over to the captured bird of prey.

"This is all a mistake," said the hawk as the farmer approached. "I was just chasing a pigeon, and the wretched bird flew right over your field. I was not going to do a bit of harm to you. Believe me, sir!"

"That may be," replied the farmer. "But unless you can tell me just what harm the pigeon had done to you, I'm afraid I'm going to have to wring your neck."

᠑᠍ *Application*: HYPOCRISY IS THE CLOAK OF VILLAINY.

THE LIONESS

ভ A GREAT RIVALRY existed among the beasts of the forest over which could produce the largest litter. Some shamefacedly admitted having only two, while others boasted proudly of having a dozen.

At last the committee called upon the lioness.

"And to how many cubs do you give birth?" they asked the proud lioness.

"One," she replied sternly, "but that one is a lion!"

ভ *Application*: QUALITY IS MORE IMPORTANT THAN QUANTITY.

MERCURY AND
THE SCULPTOR

THERE WERE TIMES when Mercury, between errands on Olympus, yearned to know whether he still was held in high esteem by mankind.

So one day, disguising himself as a traveler, he visited a sculptor's studio. Walking about among the many statues displayed there, he pointed to an image of Jupiter.

"How much are you asking for this odd piece?" he asked.

"I'll let you have that one cheap," replied the sculptor. "It is one of our less popular numbers. One drachma."

Mercury laughed in his sleeve. Then he asked: "How much for this stout lady here?"

The sculptor said: "Oh, that one is Juno. I have to get a little more for females."

Mercury's eye now caught sight of an image of himself. Thinking that as messenger of the gods and source of all commercial gain his image would command a gratifyingly high price, he said: "I see you have a very handsome statue there of Mercury. How high do you value that excellent likeness?"

"Well," replied the sculptor, "I am willing to make you a bargain. If you will pay me the price I quoted to you on the other two statues, I will throw this one in free."

&❧ *Application*: HE WHO SEEKS A COMPLIMENT SOMETIMES DISCOVERS THE TRUTH.

119

THE FARMER AND
HIS SONS

→ A FARMER, being on the point of death, called his two sons to him and said: "My sons, I am now departing from this life, but all that I have to leave you is to be found in the vineyard."

As soon as the old man was dead, the two sons, be-

lieving that their father had meant to tell them of some hidden treasure, set to work with their spades and plows and turned over the soil of the vineyard again and again. They found no treasure, it is true, but the vines, strengthened and improved by this thorough tillage, yielded a finer vintage than they ever had yielded before, and more than repaid the farmer's sons for their efforts.

෨ *Application*: INDUSTRY SOMETIMES PAYS UNEX-
PECTED DIVIDENDS.

THE BUNDLE
OF STICKS

ONCE THERE WAS a wise farmer whose quarrelsome family drove him almost to distraction. He strove in vain to reconcile his bickering sons with words of good counsel. Then one day he called his sons to his room. Before him lay a bundle of sticks which he had tied together to form a fagot.

Each one of his sons in turn was commanded by the farmer to take up the fagot and break it in two. They all tried, but tried in vain. Then, untying the bundle, the father gave them the sticks to break one by one. This, of course, they did with the greatest ease.

Then said the father: "My sons, by this example you all can see that as long as you remain united, you are a match for all your enemies. But once you quarrel and become separated, then you are destroyed."

Application: IN UNION THERE IS STRENGTH.

THE EAGLE
AND THE CROW

🐦 AN EAGLE swooped down from a high rock and pounced upon a lamb, grazing near her mother in the field. With a great beating of powerful wings he seized the lamb and flew away to his nest.

A crow sat in an oak tree watching the eagle's exploit. Said he to himself: "Surely that is an easy way to find oneself a dinner." So, spying a sturdy old ram below him, he bore down with all the force he could muster, intending to carry the ram off as a prize. He fastened his claws in the wool and tugged with all his might. But nothing happened. As a matter of fact, the ram wouldn't have known he was there if it had not been for the crow's frantic efforts to disentangle his claws from the wool.

The crow's squawking attracted the attention of the shepherd, who came up and caught him and clipped his wings and took him home to the children for a pet.

Application: IT REQUIRES MORE THAN WINGS TO BE AN EAGLE.

124

THE STAG AT
THE POOL

A STAG, one summer day, came to a pool of clear, still water to quench his thirst. As he drank he noticed his reflection in the pool and could not help admiring the image he saw there.

"I really am very handsome," said he to himself. "I should be proud of those beautiful, stately antlers. But those spindling legs and tiny feet are another matter. I wish that nature might have been more kind to me and had given me legs more worthy to bear such a noble crown."

Just at that moment the stag's sensitive nostrils scented the approach of a hunter, and even as he lingered an arrow whizzed past him. With a bound he was away, and the legs and feet of which he had just been so critical carried him speedily to a place of safety.

But once out of harm's way, the stag again fell to

musing over his appearance, and before he knew it
he had wandered into a thicket. The noble antlers
which he had so greatly admired now held him fast,
and the more he struggled the more firmly entangled
he became. Then the hunters came, and as the arrow
found its mark, he gasped: "Now that it is too late I
realize that my own vanity led to my undoing."

ʔ❖ *Application*: TOO OFTEN WE DESPISE THE VERY
THINGS THAT ARE MOST USEFUL TO
US.

THE WOLF AND
THE LAMB

AS A WOLF was lapping at the head of a running brook he spied a lamb daintily paddling his feet some distance down the stream.

"There's my supper," thought the wolf. "But I'll have to find some excuse for attacking such a harmless creature."

So he shouted down at the lamb: "How dare you

127

stir up the water I am drinking and make it muddy?"

"But you must be mistaken," bleated the lamb. "How can I be spoiling your water, since it runs from you to me and not from me to you?"

"Don't argue," snapped the wolf. "I know you. You are the one who was saying those ugly things about me behind my back a year ago."

"Oh, sir," replied the lamb, trembling, "a year ago I was not even born."

"Well," snarled the wolf, "if it was not you, then it was your father, and that amounts to the same thing. Besides, I'm not going to have you argue me out of my supper."

Without another word he fell upon the helpless lamb and tore her to pieces.

ᘺ *Application*: ANY EXCUSE WILL SERVE A TYRANT.

THE BULL AND
THE GOAT

A BULL, pursued by a lion, took shelter in a cave which was the home of a wild goat. Greatly annoyed with the intruder, the goat began to butt the tired bull with his horns. He bore the ill-treatment of the goat with patience, saying: "Because I permit you to vent your displeasure on me now does not mean that I am afraid of you. As soon as the lion is out of sight and the danger is past, then I will show you the difference between a lion and a goat."

Application: THOSE WHO TAKE TEMPORARY AD-VANTAGE OF THEIR NEIGHBORS' DIF-FICULTIES MAY LIVE TO REPENT OF THEIR INSOLENCE.

129

THE WIND AND
THE SUN

❧ A DISPUTE once arose between the wind and the sun over which was the stronger of the two. There seemed to be no way of settling the issue. But suddenly they saw a traveler coming down the road. "This is our chance," said the sun, "to prove who is right. Whichever of us can make that man take off his coat shall be the stronger. And just to show you how sure I am, I'll let you have the first chance.

So the sun hid behind a cloud, and the wind blew an icy blast. But the harder he blew the more closely did the traveler wrap his coat around him. At last the wind had to give up in disgust. Then the sun came out from behind the cloud and began to shine down upon the traveler with all his power. The traveler felt the sun's genial warmth, and as he grew warmer and warmer he began to loosen his coat. Finally he was forced to take it off altogether and to sit down in the shade of a tree and fan himself. So the sun was right, after all!

ᔓ *Application*: PERSUASION IS BETTER THAN FORCE.

THE SHEPHERD BOY
AND THE WOLF

ஃ EVERY DAY the shepherd boy was sent with his father's sheep into the mountain pasture to guard the flock. It was, indeed, a lonely spot at the edge of a dark forest, and there were no companions with whom he could pass the long, weary hours of the day.

One day, just to stir up some excitement, he rushed down from the pasture, crying "Wolf! Wolf!" The villagers heard the alarm and came running with clubs and guns to help chase the marauder away, only to find the sheep grazing peacefully and no wolf in sight.

So well had the trick worked that the foolish boy tried it again and again, and each time the villagers came running, only to be laughed at for their pains.

But there came a day when a wolf really came. The boy screamed and called for help. But all in vain! The neighbors, supposing him to be up to his old tricks, paid no heed to his cries, and the wolf devoured the sheep.

ஃ *Application*: LIARS ARE NOT BELIEVED EVEN
WHEN THEY TELL THE TRUTH

THE HEN
AND THE CAT

LL THE BARNYARD knew that the hen was indisposed. So one day the cat decided to pay her a visit of condolence. Creeping up to her nest the cat in his most sympathetic voice said: "How are you, my dear friend? I was so sorry to hear of your illness. Isn't there something that I can bring you to cheer you up and to help you feel like yourself again?"

"Thank you," said the hen. "Please be good enough to leave me in peace, and I have no fear but I shall soon be well."

Application: UNINVITED GUESTS ARE OFTEN MOST
WELCOME WHEN THEY ARE GONE.

THE WOLF AND
THE GOAT

“☞” A WOLF saw a goat browsing near the edge of a high cliff. "My dear friend," he cried in his most sympathetic voice, "aren't you afraid you will get dizzy and fall and hurt yourself?" But the goat went on feeding.

The wolf tried again. "Isn't it terribly windy up there so high with no shelter at all?" But the goat went on plucking grass.

"Besides," shouted the wolf, "I am sure that you will find the grass far sweeter and more abundant down here."

Then the goat replied: "Are you quite sure, friend wolf, that it is my dinner you are so solicitous about, and not your own?"

᠁ *Application*: BEWARE OF A FRIEND WITH AN UL-
TERIOR MOTIVE.

135

THE FARTHING
RUSHLIGHT

IN OLDEN TIMES people lighted their homes with lamps in which the pith of rushes served as wicks. There was one particular rushlight which had soaked up considerable grease and was feeling more than a little boastful.

One evening it announced before a large company that it could outshine the sun, the moon, and the stars. At that very moment a puff of wind came and blew it out. The servant who relighted it said: "Shine on, friend rushlight, and hold your tongue, there is no wind strong enough to blow out the lights of heaven."

ৡ *Application*: KNOW THY PLACE AND KEEP IT.

THE LION AND
THE MOUSE

౭❧ A LION was asleep in his den one day, when a mischievous mouse for no reason at all ran across the outstretched paw and up the royal nose of the king of beasts, awakening him from his nap. The mighty beast clapped his paw upon the now thoroughly frightened little creature and would have made an end of him.

"Please," squealed the mouse, "don't kill me. Forgive me this time, O King, and I shall never forget it. A day may come, who knows, when I may do you a good turn to repay your kindness." The lion, smiling at his little prisoner's fright and amused by the thought that so small a creature ever could be of assistance to the king of beasts, let him go.

Not long afterward the lion, while ranging the forest for his prey, was caught in the net which the hunters had set to catch him. He let out a roar that echoed through the forest. Even the mouse heard it, and recognizing the voice of his former preserver and friend, ran to the spot where he lay tangled in the net of ropes.

"Well, your majesty," said the mouse, "I know you did not believe me once when I said I would return a kindness, but here is my chance." And without further ado he set to work to nibble with his sharp little teeth at the ropes that bound the lion. Soon the lion was able to crawl out of the hunter's snare and be free.

ᏋᏉ *Application*: NO ACT OF KINDNESS, NO MATTER HOW SMALL, IS EVER WASTED.

THE BOY
AND THE NETTLE

A BOY playing in the fields one day was stung in the hand by a nettle. Running home to his mother he cried: "See what the nasty weed did to me. I barely touched it when it buried its prickers in my hand."

"It was because you touched it lightly," replied the boy's mother, "that it stung you. The next time, dear son, that you play with a nettle, grasp it tightly, and it will do you no harm."

Application: DO BOLDLY WHAT YOU DO AT ALL.

THE THIEF AND
HIS MOTHER

A SCHOOLBOY stole a hornbook from one of his fellows and brought it home to his mother. Instead of chastising him, she said: "That was very clever of you, my son." As the boy grew older he began to steal things of greater value, until at length, being caught in the very act, he was arrested, tried, found guilty, and sentenced to be hanged.

The day of his execution arrived, and he was taken from his cell and led to the gallows. In the crowd that followed the cart the thief saw his mother, weeping and beating her breast. He begged the officers to be allowed to speak one word in his sorrowing mother's ear.

When she came near and inclined her head to hear his last words he suddenly bared his teeth and bit her savagely in the lobe of her ear. All the bystanders were horrified and pushed forward with threatening gestures toward the thief. They could not understand such inhuman conduct of a son toward his mother.

Then he cried out: "You think me a brute, and I am. But I have this woman to thank for the fact that I shall soon be swinging on the gallows. She is my mother. But when I was small and did mischief, instead of punishing me, she encouraged me to my ruin. Behold an unnatural son, because when I was small I had an unnatural mother."

&ed *Application*: SPARE THE ROD AND SPOIL THE
CHILD.

141

THE EAGLE AND
THE BEETLE

A HARE, pursued by an eagle, sought refuge in the nest of a beetle whom he entreated to save him. The beetle interceded with the eagle and begged him not to break the law of sanctuary. But the eagle in his wrath gave the beetle a flop with his wing and straightway seized upon the hare and devoured him.

When the eagle flew away, the beetle flew after him in order to learn where his nest was hidden. Then one day when the eagle was away the beetle returned and rolled the eagle's eggs out of the nest, one by one, and broke them. Grieved and enraged that anyone should attempt so audacious a thing, the eagle built his nest in a higher place. But again his eggs suffered a similar fate.

In desperation the eagle flew up to Jupiter, his

lord and king, and placed the third brood of eggs, as a sacred deposit, in his lap, begging him to guard them from harm. But the beetle, having made a little ball of dirt, flew up with it and dropped it in Jupiter's lap. The god, rising quickly to shake it off, and forgetting the eggs, dropped them and they were broken.

Jupiter, knowing that the beetle was in the right, but loath to see the race of eagles diminished, used his good offices to persuade the beetle to call a truce with the eagle. This the beetle would not agree to do, and Jupiter was forced to transfer the eagle's breeding to another season, when there were no beetles to be seen.

Application: THE LAWS OF HOSPITALITY ARE NOT TO BE BROKEN WITH IMPUNITY.

THE TWO POTS

ॐ TWO POTS, one of earthenware and the other of brass, were carried downstream by a river in flood. The brass pot begged his companion to remain as close by his side as possible, and he would protect him.

"You are very kind," replied the earthen pot, "but that is just what I am afraid of. If you will only keep your distance, I shall be able to float down in safety. But should we come too close, whether I strike you or you strike me, I am sure to be the one who will get the worst of it."

ॐ *Application*: AVOID TOO POWERFUL NEIGHBORS.

THE YOUNG MAN AND
THE SWALLOW

෮ A FOOLISH MAN received his inheritance from his father, and lost no time in spending it in gambling and riotous living.

The day the last of his substance was lost he was walking along the road. It was wintertime, but the sun was shining and it was unseasonably warm. A foolish swallow, pretending that it was spring, flew gaily around in the sky.

"It looks as though spring was here," said the foolish man. "I won't be needing all these clothes." So he pawned them, gambled with the proceeds, and lost.

But now, when he left the town, the sun was gone. Snow lay on the ground, and everything was frozen hard. The foolish swallow, frozen stiff, lay dead in the snow. Looking at the dead bird, the shivering man said with chattering teeth: "It is all your fault that I am in this unhappy fix!"

෮ *Application*: THERE IS NO PROFIT IN BLAMING YOUR FOOLISH MISTAKES ON FOOL-ISH ADVISERS.

THE WOLF
AND THE CRANE

A WOLF, in gorging himself upon some poor animal he had killed, had got a small bone stuck in his throat. The pain was terrible, and he ran up and down beseeching every animal he met to relieve him. None of the animals, however, felt very sorry for the wolf, for, as one of them put it, "That bone which is stuck in the wolf's throat might just as well be one of mine."

Finally the suffering wolf met the crane. "I'll give you anything," he whined, "if you will help take this bone out of my throat."

The crane, moved by his entreaties and promises of reward, ventured her long neck down the wolf's throat and drew out the bone. She then modestly asked for the promised reward.

"Reward?" barked the wolf, showing his teeth.

"Of all the ungrateful creatures! I have permitted you to live to tell your grandchildren that you put your head in a wolf's mouth without having it bitten off, and then you ask for a reward! Get out of here before I change my mind!"

Application: THOSE WHO LIVE ON EXPECTATION ARE SURE TO BE DISAPPOINTED.

147

THE COUNTRY MOUSE
AND THE
TOWN MOUSE

ONCE UPON A TIME a country mouse who had a friend in town invited him, for old acquaintance's sake, to pay him a visit in the country. Though plain and rough and somewhat frugal in his nature, the country mouse opened his heart and store in honor of an old friend. There was not a carefully stored-up morsel that he did not produce from his larder—peas and barley, cheese parings and nuts—to please the palate of his city-bred guest.

The town mouse, however, turned up his long nose at the rough country fare. "How is it, my friend," he exclaimed, "that you can endure the boredom of living like a toad in a hole? You can't really prefer these solitary rocks and woods to the excitement of the city. You are wasting your time out here

148

in the wilderness. A mouse, you know, does not live forever, one must make the most of life while it lasts. So come with me and I'll show you life and the town."

In the end, the country mouse allowed himself to be persuaded, and the two friends set out together on their journey to town. It was late in the evening when they crept stealthily into the city, and midnight before they reached the great house where the town mouse lived.

On the table of the splendid banquet room were the remains of a lavish feast. It was now the turn of the city mouse to play host. He ran to and fro to supply all the guest's wants. He pressed dish upon dish and dainty upon dainty upon him as though he were waiting on a king. The country mouse, for his part, pretended to feel quite at home, and blessed

149

the good fortune that had wrought such a change in his way of life.

But in the midst of his enjoyment, just as he was beginning to feel contempt for his frugal life in the country, the sound of barking and growling could be heard outside the door.

"What is that?" said the country mouse.

"Oh, that is only the master's dogs," replied the town mouse.

"Only!" replied the visitor in dismay. "I can't say that I like music with my dinner."

At that moment the door flew open and a party of revelers, together with two huge dogs, burst into the room. The affrighted friends jumped from the table and concealed themselves in a far corner of the chamber. At length, when things seemed quiet, the country mouse stole out from his hiding place, and bidding his friend good-bye, whispered in his ear: "This fine way of living may do for those who like it. But give me my barley bread in peace and in security in preference to your dainty fare partaken with fear and trembling."

ଚ୬ *Application*: A CRUST EATEN IN PEACE IS BETTER THAN A BANQUET PARTAKEN IN ANXIETY.

150

THE FARMER
AND THE STORK

૨૭ A FARMER, who was tired of having his newly planted corn stolen by the cranes, set a net in his field. When he went to examine his snare he found that he had caught several of them, and included in their number was a stork.

"Please, sir," begged the stork, "don't kill me. I am not one of these greedy cranes who eat all your corn. I am a good and pious bird. I take care of my aged parents. I—"

But the farmer cut him short. "All that you say about yourself may be true. All I know, however, is that I have caught you with those who were destroying my crops, and I'm afraid that you will have to suffer the same fate as those in whose company you were captured."

ॐ *Application*: YOU ARE JUDGED BY THE COMPANY YOU KEEP.

THE MAN AND
THE LION

ONCE UPON A TIME a man and a lion met on the highway, and for some distance journeyed along together quite agreeably. But when the conversation began to concern which creature was superior, a man or a lion, the dispute waxed warmer and warmer.

They were passing a statue which depicted Hercules strangling a lion. "See there!" said the man. "That statue proves that I am right. What stronger proof of man's superiority over a lion could you ask?"

"That doesn't prove a thing," retorted the lion. "Just let us lions be the sculptors and every statue will show a lion standing over a man!"

ॐ *Application*: WE ARE BUT SORRY WITNESSES IN
OUR OWN CAUSE.

THE LION
AND HIS THREE
COUNSELORS

꿈 THE KING OF BEASTS was in an irritable mood. That morning his mate had told him that his breath was most unpleasant. After doing considerable roaring to prove that he was king he summoned his counselors.

First he called the sheep.

"Friend sheep," he roared, opening wide his great mouth, "would you say that my breath smells unpleasant?"

Believing that the lion wanted an honest answer, the sheep gave it, and the king of beasts bit off her head for a fool.

Then he called the wolf and asked him the same question. The wolf, catching sight of the carcass of the sheep, said: "Why, your majesty, you have a breath as sweet as blossoms in the spring—"

Before he could finish he had been torn to pieces for a flatterer.

At last the lion called the fox and put the question to him. The fox gave a hollow cough, then cleared his throat. "Your majesty," he whispered, "truly, I have such a cold in the head that I cannot smell at all."

&❧ *Application*: IN DANGEROUS TIMES WISE MEN SAY NOTHING.

THE STAG IN THE
OX STALL

A STAG closely pursued by a pack of hounds sought refuge in the stable of a farmer. Trembling with fear he entered an empty ox stall where he tried to conceal himself under the straw. Only the stag's horns remained in sight. But the stable was dark, and when the hunters came along and asked whether anyone had seen the stag the stableboys looked, but could see nothing.

The stag began to take courage because he had not been discovered and thought that with the coming of darkness he would be able to make his escape.

"Don't be too sure," said one of the oxen in an adjoining stall. "When the master has finished his supper he will come to see that all is safe for the night. And then I fear that your life will be in jeopardy, for the master has eyes in the back of his head."

156

Even as he spoke, the farmer entered the stable. Pointing to the mount of straw, he called to the stableboys: "What are these two curious things sticking up out of the straw?" And when the stableboys came the stag was discovered and captured.

ತ Application: THERE IS NO EYE LIKE THE
                          MASTER'S.

THE FOX
AND THE WOODMAN

A FOX, hard pressed by a pack of hounds who had been chasing him over hill and dale, came up to a man who was cutting wood outside his cottage.

"Please, kind sir," panted the weary fox, "will you hide me in a corner where I will be safe from the hunters' hounds who wish to kill me?"

The man showed him his own hut, and the fox, creeping in, hid himself in a corner. Presently the hunters came up.

"Have you seen a fox hereabouts?" they asked.

"Why, no," replied the woodman. "I have been chopping wood here all morning." As he spoke he pointed with his finger to the very corner of the cottage where the fox was hiding. The hunters, not knowing what he meant, called their dogs and rode away.

As soon as the danger was past the fox sneaked out of his hiding place and would have departed without a word of thanks.

"Just a moment, there, friend fox," the woodman said. "Is this the way you take leave of your host, without even a thank you for saving your life?"

"A pretty host!" snapped the fox. "If you had been as honest with your finger as you were with your tongue, then I should not have left your roof without bidding you farewell."

ᔆ *Application*: THERE IS AS MUCH MALICE IN A WINK AS IN A WORD.

THE LION
AND OTHER BEASTS
GO HUNTING

THE LION preferred to hunt alone, but now and then he would invite other beasts to accompany him. Upon one such occasion, the hunters cornered and killed a fat stag.

Taking a commanding position before the dead stag, the lion roared: "Beasts, it is time to divide the spoils. I demand that it be quartered. The first quarter shall fall to me as king of the beasts. The second is mine as arbiter. A third quarter is due me for my part in the chase. Now, as for the fourth part—" and here the lion gave an ominous growl—"let him take it who dares!"

&ampApplication: MANY MAY SHARE IN THE LABORS
BUT NOT IN THE SPOILS.

THE SICK LION

ʔ THE LION allowed word to get around that he was on his deathbed and wished all the animals of his kingdom to come to his cave to hear his last will and testament.

The fox, who lived by his wits, did not wish to be the first to enter the cave. So he lingered near the entrance while the goat and the sheep and the calf went in to receive the last wishes of the king of beasts.

After a time, the lion seemed to make a remarkable recovery, and came to the mouth of the cave. Seeing the fox a safe distance away, he bellowed: "Why do you not come in to pay your respects to me, friend fox?"

"Please pardon me, your majesty," replied the fox, "but I did not wish to crowd you. I noticed the tracks of many of your subjects going into your cave, but so far I have seen none coming out. Until some of them come out, and there is more room in the cave, I think I'll stay out here in the open air."

ʔ *Application*: DON'T BELIEVE ALL YOU HEAR.

THE MULE

҉ A MULE had been having an easy time of it with nothing to do but eat. One day as he was frisking about the pasture he began to fancy himself a runner.

"My mother was a famous race horse. I'll bet I can run as fast as ever she could," he said to himself. And to prove it he set off at what he thought was a fast pace toward the barn.

Not so long afterward the mule's master found it necessary to get to the village in a great hurry. Jumping upon the animal's back the farmer began to flog him and urge him to greater speed, until the mule, gasping for breath, said: "My mother may have been a race horse, but my father was only a jackass."

Application: EVERY TRUTH HAS TWO SIDES.

THE NURSE
AND THE WOLF

I F YOU DON'T stop crying this instant," said an old nurse to the child who sat screaming on her lap, "I will throw you out the window to the wolf."

At that very moment a wolf happened to be passing under the window and heard what the nurse had said. So he sat down to wait, saying to himself: "This must be my lucky day. From the way that baby is crying, my dinner ought to be coming out that window any minute now."

He waited and he waited. The baby stopped crying and went to sleep, and nothing happened. All through the cold night the wolf sat there, his mouth watering whenever he thought of the dainty morsel.

He was tired and stiff from sitting in one position. Then, toward morning, the glad sound of a baby crying came from the window again.

Rushing to the window he looked up at the nurse and wagged his tail. But all the old nurse did was to shut the window with a bang and set the dogs upon the hungry wolf.

As he trotted away the wolf said to himself: "Next time I won't believe all I hear."

Application: ENEMIES' PROMISES ARE MADE TO BE BROKEN.

THE TRAVELERS
AND THE BEAR

TWO MEN were traveling together in a wild and lonely part of the country. Before they had set out on their journey they had promised that if any danger should overtake them they would stand by each other to the death.

They had gone only a short way when a bear rushed out of the bushes and made straight for them. One of the men, quick as a flash, took to a tree and scrambled up into its branches. The other, seeing he had no time to escape, threw himself flat upon the ground, pretending to be dead.

As he lay there in the dust holding his breath the bear came near, sniffing and smelling, and putting his muzzle close to the man's ear. Then, at last, with a growl he shook his head and lumbered away, for bears will not touch a dead body.

167

When the animal was completely out of sight the man in the tree slid down to the ground, and somewhat shamefacedly approached his companion, who now was sitting on a stone.

"Well, old fellow," he said, "that was a close one, wasn't it? By the way, didn't I see that bear whispering to you? What did he say when he put his mouth to your ear?"

"Why," replied the other, looking his companion straight in the eye, "it was no great secret. He just told me that the next time I should not place any faith in the word of a cowardly knave like you."

ટ✿ *Application*: DON'T TRUST A FRIEND WHO IS LIABLE TO DESERT YOU WHEN TROUBLE COMES.

THE FATHER AND HIS
TWO DAUGHTERS

૨ A MAN WHO had two daughters gave one in marriage to a gardener and the other to a potter. After the weddings the daughters departed with their husbands to their new homes, and the father was left alone.

The following spring the father went to visit the daughter who married the gardener. "How fares it with you, daughter?" he asked.

"Very well, indeed," she replied. "We have everything we want. I have but one wish. And that is that we have a heavy shower to water all our growing plants."

Later the father visited the daughter who had married the potter. "And how is everything with you, daughter?" he inquired.

"There is not a thing we lack," said she. "My only hope is that this fine weather and hot sun may continue so that all our tiles may be baked."

"Alas," said the father, "if you must have fine weather and your sister must have rain, what am I to pray for myself?"

૨ *Application*: YOU CAN'T PLEASE EVERYBODY.

THE TORTOISE
AND THE EAGLE

THE TORTOISE once upon a time was not the contented fellow that he is today. There was a time when he wished with all his heart that he could fly. As he watched the birds disporting themselves in the clouds he felt sure that if he could get up into the air he could soar with the best of them.

One day he called to an eagle who was hovering overhead: "Friend eagle, you are the best flier among all the birds. If you will teach me to fly I will bring you all the treasures of the sea."

The eagle replied: "But you are asking the impossible, friend tortoise. In the first place, you have no wings and, in the second, nature never intended you to fly."

But the tortoise kept pleading and promising greater and greater rewards. So finally the eagle said that he would do the best he could. Telling the tortoise to hang on, he bore him high into the sky. Then he loosed his hold upon the now thoroughly frightened tortoise and cried: "All right, start flying."

The poor tortoise, however, dropped like a plummet and was dashed to pieces on the rocks below.

ટ Application: VANITY CARRIES ITS OWN PUNISHMENT.

THE DOG
INVITED TO SUPPER

A GENTLEMAN, having prepared a great feast, invited his good friend to supper. It chanced that on that same day the gentleman's dog met the friend's dog. "Come," said he, "my good fellow, and sup with us tonight."

The dog was delighted with the invitation, and as he stood watching the dinner being brought from the kitchen, he licked his chops and said: "My, but that smells good. This is luck, indeed! I shall make the most of my opportunity and eat my fill tonight, for I may have nothing to eat tomorrow."

As he spoke thus to himself he wagged his tail and gave a sly look at his friend who had invited him. But his tail wagging to and fro caught the attention of the cook, who, seeing a stranger, straightway seized him by the legs and threw him out the window.

172

When he reached the ground he set off yelping down the street. Thereupon the neighbors' dogs ran up to him and asked him how he had enjoyed his supper. "To tell you the truth," said he with a sorry smile, "we drank so deep that I can't even tell you which way I got out of the house."

ɞ *Application*: THEY WHO ENTER BY THE BACK STAIRS MAY EXPECT TO BE SHOWN OUT AT THE WINDOW.

THE MOUNTEBANK
AND THE FARMER

꒰ A HUGE CROWD had gathered to watch the performance of the famous mountebank. According to rumor, he had come with an act so new and so miraculous that its like had never before been seen on any stage.

The curtains parted, and there stood the artist alone upon the stage without any assistants or apparatus of any kind. Curiosity and suspense kept the audience in complete silence. You could have heard a pin drop. Suddenly the mountebank thrust his head into his cloak, and so cleverly mimicked the squeaking of a young pig that the audience insisted he had one concealed somewhere about him. But when he was searched no pig could be found.

Just then a farmer stood up and bellowed: "Do you call that a pig's squeak? If you folks want to hear what a pig's squeak is really like, then come around here tomorrow!"

The next day found a great crowd assembled. They had come to see the clever mountebank put the boasting farmer to shame. Both men appeared on the stage. First the clown gave some most realistic grunts and squeals while the crowd roared and applauded.

Then the farmer put his head down into his cloak, and immediately hideous squeals came forth.

"Booh, booh!" yelled the crowd. "That sounds no more like a pig than a cow! We want the mountebank! Get off the stage, you country lout! Who taught you to squeal? Get back to your barnyard!"

But the farmer stood his ground. "You fools," he cried, "this is what you ignoramuses have been hissing!" And he drew from his cloak a real live little pig whose ear he had been pinching to make him squeal. "The next time, my smart city friends, let your own senses help you to judge instead of your pretty prejudices!"

&> *Application*: DO NOT DENOUNCE THE GENUINE, ONLY TO APPLAUD AN IMITATION.

THE DOG
AND THE SHADOW

ONE DAY a dog stole a piece of meat out of a butcher shop, and on his way to a safe place where he could eat it without interruption he had to cross a footbridge over a clear stream. Looking down he saw his own reflection in the water.

Thinking that the reflection was another dog with another piece of meat, and being a greedy dog, he made up his mind to have that also. So he snarled and made a grab for the other dog's meat.

As his greedy mouth opened, out dropped the piece of meat and fell into the stream and was lost.

Application: GRASP AT THE SHADOW AND LOSE THE SUBSTANCE.

THE OLD MAN
AND DEATH

AN OLD MAN, stooped by age and hard work, was gathering sticks in the forest. As he hobbled painfully along he thought of his troubles and began to feel very sorry for himself.

With a hopeless gesture he threw his bundle of sticks upon the ground and groaned: "Life is too hard. I cannot bear it any longer. If only Death would come and take me!"

Even as the words were out of his mouth Death, in the form of a skeleton in a black robe, stood before him. "I heard you call me, sir," he said. "What can I do for you?"

"Please, sir," replied the old man, "could you please help me put this bundle of sticks back on my shoulder again?"

⇢ *Application*: HOW SORRY WE WOULD BE IF MANY
OF OUR WISHES WERE GRANTED.

THE MOUSE AND
THE FROG

I T WAS an evil day for the mouse when he made
the acquaintance of a frog on the eve of a journey
into the country. Protesting his great affection, the
frog persuaded the mouse to allow him to go along.
But we shall never know what possessed the mouse
when he let the frog tie one of his own forefeet to one
of the frog's hindfeet, for surely it made traveling
most uncomfortable indeed.

However, they limped and hopped along the path
until they came to a stream of water. The frog immediately jumped in, saying: "Follow me, friend
mouse, and have no fear. You may find the harness a
bit awkward, but remember that I'll be right by your
side as we swim across."

So they began to swim. Scarcely had they reached
midstream, however, when the frog took a sudden

179

plunge to the bottom, dragging the unfortunate mouse after him. The struggling and threshing of the mouse caused such a great commotion in the water that it attracted the attention of a hawk sailing in the sky overhead. Swift as lightning he pounced down upon the drowning mouse and carried him away. And with them, of course, went the frog as well.

ॐ *Application*: HE WHO COMPASSES THE DESTRUC- TION OF HIS NEIGHBOR OFTEN IS CAUGHT IN HIS OWN SNARE.

THE OAK AND
THE REED

꒰❧ A PROUD OAK grew upon the bank of a stream. For a full hundred years it had withstood the buffeting of the winds, but one day there came a violent storm. The great oak fell with a mighty crash into the swollen river and was carried down toward the sea.

Later the oak tree came to rest on the shore where some reeds were growing. The tree was amazed to see the reeds standing upright.

"How ever did you manage to weather that terrible storm?" he asked. "I have stood up against many a storm, but this one was too strong for me."

"That's just it," replied the reed. "All these years you have stubbornly pitted your great strength against the wind. You were too proud to yield a little. I, on the other hand, knowing my weakness, just bend and let the wind blow over me without trying to resist it. The harder the wind blows the more I humble myself, so here I am!"

꒰❧ *Application*: IT IS BETTER TO BEND THAN TO BREAK.

THE SWALLOW'S
ADVICE

A FARMER was sowing his field with hemp seeds while a swallow and some other birds sat on the fence watching him.

"Beware of that man," said the swallow solemnly.

"Why should we be afraid of him?" asked the other birds.

"That farmer is sowing hemp seed," replied the swallow. "It is most important that you pick up every seed that he drops. You will live to regret it if you don't."

But, of course, the silly birds paid no heed to the swallow's advice. So, with the coming of the spring rains, the hemp grew up. And one day the hemp was made into cord, and of the cord nets were made. And many of the birds that had despised the swallow's advice were caught in the nets made of the very hemp that was grown from the seeds they had failed to pick up.

Application: UNLESS THE SEED OF EVIL IS DE-STROYED IT WILL GROW UP TO DE-STROY US.

THE OLD WOMAN
AND
THE PHYSICIAN

AN OLD WOMAN, who had become blind, summoned a physician.

"Since you are a healer of such great renown," said she, "I would like to strike a bargain with you. If you will restore my eyesight I will give you a most handsome reward. But if, within a reasonable time, you fail and my malady still remains, then you shall receive nothing."

The physician, observing that the old woman was comfortably off and had many possessions, concluded the agreement. So he called regularly and pretended to treat the woman's eyes, meanwhile, bit by bit, carrying off all her goods.

After a time, whatever had been causing the old lady's blindness disappeared, and she found her sight again. Thereupon the physician demanded the stipulated fee. But discovering that nearly all of her possessions had disappeared since the coming of the physician, she kept putting him off with excuses. At length he grew impatient and had his patient summoned before a judge.

When called upon for her defense, the old woman said: "What this man says is true enough. I promised to give him his fee if my sight were restored, but nothing if my eyes remained blind. Now, then, he says that I am cured, but it cannot be true. For before my malady came upon me I could see all sorts of furniture and goods in my house. But now I cannot see a single stick, yet he tells me that he has restored my sight!"

ð❧ *Application*: HE WHO PLAYS A TRICK MUST BE PREPARED TO TAKE A JOKE.

THE EAGLE
AND THE ARROW

ONE DAY a bowman saw an eagle soaring lazily in the sky. Quickly he notched an arrow and sent it whizzing after the bird. It found its mark, and the eagle felt itself wounded to death. As it slowly fluttered down to earth it saw that the haft of the arrow which had pierced its breast was fitted with one of its own feathers.

Application: HOW OFTEN DO WE SUPPLY OUR ENE-MIES WITH THE MEANS OF OUR OWN DESTRUCTION!

186

THE THIEF
AND THE BOY

A BOY WAS PLAYING by the well curb when a thief came walking by. Suddenly the boy began to cry. His little shoulders heaved with his sobbing. His wailing could be heard for a mile or more. When his grief had abated somewhat the thief said: "Why all the tears, my little friend?"

"Oh, dear, oh, dear," whimpered the boy. "I was playing with my beautiful silver mug. B-b-but the string broke and it fell down into the well."

"That's easy," replied the thief. Tossing off his clothes he let himself down into the well. It was his intention to recover the valuable mug and keep it for himself.

Down, down, down he went. Colder and colder grew the water, but he couldn't find the mug—for the simple reason that there wasn't any! After a while the thief began to realize that the boy, having recognized him for a thief, had sent him down into the well to get him out of the way.

Painfully he climbed out of the well, shivering with the cold. When he reached the top again both the boy and the thief's clothes were gone.

ટ≫ *Application*: HE WHO TRIES TO OUTSMART HIS NEIGHBOR WINDS UP BY OUTSMART- ING HIMSELF.

188

THE FIR TREE
AND THE BRAMBLE

ভ A FIR TREE which grew tall and straight over most of the forest trees was boasting one day to a humble bramble bush beneath him. His haughtiness and boasting made the bramble bush annoyed, and he said: "If I were as tall as you I would not need to put on such airs."

"How can a wretched bramble bush understand the feelings of a tree whose top brushes the clouds," was the haughty reply.

"Just wait," said the bramble. "I hope I am here the day the woodmen come with their sharp axes and saws looking for a tall fir tree. Then, I wager, you will wish you were nothing but a humble, useless bramble bush."

ভ *Application*: THE HUMBLE ARE SECURE FROM MANY DANGERS TO WHICH THE PROUD ARE SUBJECT.

189

THE VAIN CROW

⭕ ONE DAY a vain crow found some feathers which a peacock had shed. Sticking them among his own rusty black ones, he began to strut about ignoring and despising his old friends and companions.

Dressed in his borrowed plumage, he very cockily sought out a flock of peacocks who were walking with stately steps on the park lawn. Instantly detecting the true nature of the intruder, they stripped him of his finery and falling upon him with their sharp beaks, they sent him packing.

The bedraggled crow, sadder but wiser, betook himself to his former companions, and would have been satisfied to associate with them again. But the crows, remembering how obnoxious he had been with his airs and his vanity, drummed him out of their society. One of those whom he had so lately despised offered him the following advice: "Be contented with what nature made you and you will avoid the contempt of your peers and the punishment of your betters."

ଓ *Application*: HAPPINESS IS NOT TO BE FOUND IN BORROWED FINERY.

191

THE TWO
CRABS

A MOTHER CRAB and her child were strolling along the beach one day. It was a fine morning, but the mother crab was too busy scolding her offspring to pay any attention to the weather.

"Why in the world, child, do you not walk as the other creatures do—forward instead of backward?" she complained.

"Mother, dear," replied the little crab, "do but set the example, yourself, and I will follow you."

ह्र *Application*: EXAMPLE IS THE BEST PRECEPT.

THE MOUNTAIN
IN LABOR

 কৈ ONE DAY the people of a certain country heard a mighty rumbling in the near-by mountain. Smoke was pouring from the summit. The earth was trembling, and great rocks came hurtling down into the valley. The mountain seemed to be in labor, and all the people rushed to a vantage point where they could see what terrible thing was about to happen.

They waited and waited, while the sky grew dark and the rumblings and thunderings increased. Finally, as the people watched, there was one earthquake more violent than all the others. Suddenly, a huge fissure appeared in the side of the mountain. The people threw themselves down upon their knees. Some of them fainted. All the rest waited with bated breath to see what would happen next.

The thundering stopped. A deep silence fell. And out of the gap in the side of the mountain popped a mouse!

 কৈ *Application*: MAGNIFICENT PROMISES OFTEN END IN PALTRY PERFORMANCES.

THE FISHERMAN
PIPING

꩜ THERE WAS ONCE a fisherman who enjoyed playing on the bagpipes as much as he did fishing. He sat down on the riverbank and played a gay tune, hoping that the fish would be attracted and jump ashore.

194

When nothing happened, he took a casting net, threw it into the water, and soon drew it forth filled with fish. Then, as the fish danced and flopped about in the net on shore, the fisherman shook his head and said: "Since you would not dance when I piped, I will have none of your dancing now."

᠎ *Application*: TO DO THE RIGHT THING AT THE RIGHT SEASON IS A GREAT ART.

195

THE MAN AND
HIS TWO WIVES

৪৯ BACK IN THE DAYS when a man was allowed more wives than one, a middle-aged bachelor whose hair was only just beginning to turn gray fell in love with two women at one time, and married both of them.

One was young and blooming, and wished her husband to appear as youthful as herself. So every night she would comb his hair, and as she did so she would pull out all the gray hairs.

The other wife, who was older, saw her husband growing gray with pleasure, for she did not like to be mistaken for his mother. So each morning when she brushed his hair she would industriously pluck out every black hair she could find.

For a time the man enjoyed the attention and devotion of his wives, until one morning when he looked into the mirror and found that he was completely bald.

৪৯ *Application*: YIELD TO THE CAPRICES OF ALL AND YOU SOON WILL HAVE NOTHING TO YIELD AT ALL.

THE OLD WOMAN
AND HER MAIDS

A THRIFTY OLD WOMAN kept two serving maids to help her with the housework. The two maids slept together in the loft, and it was their old mistress's custom to rouse them up at cockcrow.

Naturally, the maidservants disliked very much being awakened before daylight every morning. They decided that if they could prevent the cock from giving his alarm each morning they would be able to lie longer in bed. The opportunity came, and the cock's neck was wrung. But, lo and behold, the next night, the old woman, missing her usual alarm, and being afraid of oversleeping, climbed up into the loft with her candle and awakened the sleeping maids at midnight.

ᶜ᷾ᵛ *Application*: TOO MUCH CUNNING OVERREACHES ITSELF.

197

THE MONKEY
AND
THE DOLPHIN

&⟩ IT WAS an old custom among sailors to take with them on their voyages monkeys and other pets to amuse them while they were at sea. So it happened that on a certain voyage a sailor took with him a monkey as a companion on board ship.

Off the coast of Sunium, the famous promontory of Attica, the ship was caught in a violent storm and was wrecked. All on board were thrown into the water and had to swim for land as best they could. And among them was the monkey.

A dolphin saw him struggling in the waves, and taking him for a man, went to his assistance. As they were nearing the shore just opposite Piraeus, the harbor of Athens, the dolphin spoke. "Are you an Athenian?" he asked.

"Yes, indeed," replied the monkey, as he spat out

a mouthful of sea water. "I belong to one of the first families of the city."

"Then, of course, you know Piraeus," said the dolphin.

"Oh, yes," said the monkey, who thought Piraeus must be the name of some distinguished citizen, "he is one of my very dearest friends."

Disgusted by so obvious a falsehood, the dolphin dived to the bottom of the sea and left the monkey to his fate.

Application: THOSE WHO PRETEND TO BE WHAT THEY ARE NOT, SOONER OR LATER, FIND THEMSELVES IN DEEP WATER.

THE WILD BOAR
AND THE FOX

A WILD BOAR was busily whetting his tusks against a tree in the forest when a fox came by.

"Why are you wasting your time in this manner?" asked the fox. "Neither a hunter nor a hound is in sight, and no danger is at hand."

"True enough," replied the boar; "but when the danger does arise, I shall have something else to do than to sharpen my weapons."

ᔔ *Application*: IT IS TOO LATE TO WHET THE SWORD WHEN THE TRUMPET SOUNDS.

THE TREES
AND THE AX

ᓵ A WOODMAN came into the forest one day carrying an ax without any handle! He sat down upon the mossy ground and looked about him rather helplessly.

"What's the trouble, friend woodman?" inquired a friendly old oak.

"I need a handle for my ax," replied the man. "Most any piece of wood will do."

After a whispered consultation, the trees good-naturedly offered the woodman a fine piece of tough ashwood for a handle.

But no sooner had the woodchopper fitted the helve with his ax when he set to work on all sides, felling the noblest trees in the wood.

The old oak, witnessing the destruction all about him, whispered to the cedar tree: "If we had not sacrificed our humble neighbor, the ash tree, to please the woodchopper, we might all of us remain standing for ages."

ᓵ *Application*: THEY ARE FOOLISH WHO GIVE THEIR ENEMY THE MEANS OF DESTROYING THEM.

201

THE MOUSE AND
THE WEASEL

> **A LITTLE** MOUSE, who had gone without food for days and was almost starved, had the good fortune to come upon a basket of corn. Weak as he was, he was able to make his way into the basket, where he stuffed and gorged himself to his heart's content. His hunger appeased, the mouse decided to

go home, only to find to his dismay that his enlarged belly would not go through the hole in the basket.

So there he sat bewailing his fate, until a weasel, brought to the spot by the mouse's squeaks, said to him: "Stop your weeping and wailing, friend mouse. The thing for you to do is to fast where you are until you are thin again. When you reduce yourself to the same condition you were in when you entered, then you can get out the same way."

ॐ *Application*: DON'T COVET MORE THAN YOU CAN CARRY.

203

THE LION AND
THE ASS
GO HUNTING

As EVERYONE KNOWS, the lion is a mighty hunter. But even the king of beasts at times grows tired of hunting for his food. So once a lion made an agreement with an ass to go hunting together.

The plan was that they were to proceed to a certain cave where a herd of wild goats were accustomed to take shelter. The lion was to take a position near the mouth of the cave while the ass went inside and made such a hideous noise by braying and kicking and stamping that the terrified animals would run right into the lion's trap.

The plan worked beautifully. The lion caught and killed and devoured several goats, and after his hearty meal he stretched out to take his ease.

Just then the ass, anxious to claim his share of the noble victory, came up to the reclining lion and said: "How was that for a job? Didn't I give those goats the worst of it? And what do you think of the noise I made? Wasn't it wonderful?"

"Yes, indeed," replied the lion sleepily. "As a matter of fact if I hadn't known you to be only an ass I think I would have been scared myself."

𝄢 *Application*: BRAGGARTS USUALLY GET THEMSELVES LAUGHED AT IN THE END.

205

THE FOX AND
THE BRAMBLE

ಶಿ THE HOUNDS were in full cry in pursuit of the wily fox and were gaining on him rapidly. Turning suddenly from his course, the fox dived through a hedge that was full of sharp thorns.

"Those dogs will never follow me through these brambles," said the fox to himself.

Just then he stepped on one of the thorns.

"That was a dirty trick," he snarled. "What kind of bramble are you? Here I come to you for help, but you only stab me for my pains."

"Wait a minute, friend fox," replied the bramble. "I'm the one who should be angry. You came running to me for help with your tail between your legs. I didn't ask you to come this way, did I? You knew I had thorns, and you were perfectly willing to have the dogs wounded by them. Now that you, yourself, got caught on one of them you complain. Next time I hope the hounds catch you!"

All that the fox could do was lick his smarting paw.

ࡥ *Application*: TO THE SELFISH ALL ARE SELFISH.

THE TWO
FROGS

ALL SUMMER LONG there had been no rain, and all the lakes and streams had dried up. Two frogs, looking for water, came upon a deep well. They sat down and argued as to whether they should dive in or not.

Said one frog: "My, but that water looks good down there! I think we should hop in without delay. Not only will we have plenty of good fresh water, but we'll have it all to ourselves."

"What you say may be true," said the second frog, "but suppose this well dries up too? Then where will we be—no water and no way of getting out either!"

⁊ *Application*: THINK TWICE BEFORE YOU LEAP!

THE TRAVELERS
AND THE HATCHET

ॐ TWO MEN were traveling along the highroad toward the town. Suddenly one of them spied a hatchet half hidden in the fallen leaves.

"Look what I have found!" he cried, picking up the tool.

"Do not say '*I*,'" replied his companion. "It is more proper to say, 'Look what *we* have found!'"

The finder of the hatchet shrugged his shoulders, and they continued on their way. Presently they came upon a group of men whose eyes were on the roadway as though they were looking for something. Suddenly one of the strangers pointed to the approaching twain, and they rushed up to them, pointing to the hatchet.

"Alas," said the traveler who had found the hatchet, "it looks as though we are in trouble."

"What do you mean '*we* are in trouble'? What you really mean to say is that '*I* am in trouble!'"

ॐ *Application*: HE WHO WILL NOT ALLOW HIS FRIEND TO SHARE THE PRIZE MUST NOT EXPECT HIM TO SHARE THE DANGER.

THE HORSE
AND THE LION

THE LION was hungry. Hunting had not been too good during the past week. He was sitting by the roadside feeling sorry for himself when a handsome horse came trotting past. The lion's mouth watered as he thought what a wonderful dinner that horse would make if only he could catch him.

The lion just couldn't get his mind off that horse. So he let it be noised about that he had become a wonderful doctor who could heal any animal's complaint.

A day or two later the horse, pretending that he had a thorn in one hoof, came to the lion's den for help. The lion licked his chops. This was the chance he had been looking for. He asked the horse to raise one of his hind feet so he could make an examination.

Solicitously, in his best bedside manner, he bent his head as though to examine the ailing hoof.

Just as he was ready to spring, the horse let go with his upraised hoof. There was a sickening thud as hoof met nose. And the last thing the lion remembered was a whinny of laughter as the horse galloped away toward the forest.

ટ᠊ঌ *Application*: THE BEST LAID-OUT SCHEME OFTEN HAS A KICKBACK.

THE FIGHTING COCKS
AND
THE EAGLE

ã TWO YOUNG fighting cocks were battling fiercely to see which of them would be the barnyard champion. At last the one that was beaten crept into a corner to hide his wounds and his shame.

But the conqueror flapped his wings and crowed lustily. Then he flew up to the top of the house where he continued to flap his wings and crow so that everyone would be sure to know who was victor. Just then an eagle, sailing by overhead, spied the crowing cock. Swooping down he seized him in his talons and carried him off for dinner. Meanwhile the defeated rival came out from his hiding place and took possession of the barnyard over which they had contended.

Application: PRIDE GOETH BEFORE A FALL.

213

THE BIRDS, THE BEASTS, AND THE BAT

ONCE UPON A TIME war broke out between the birds and the beasts of the earth. For a long while the issue of the battle was uncertain. The bat, taking advantage of the fact that he had certain characteristics of both, kept aloof and remained neutral.

The birds said, "Come with us." But he shook his head and said, "I am a beast." Later some of the animals approached him and asked him to join their side. "I am a bird," said he.

In due course, a peace was concluded between the embattled birds and beasts. So the bat flew blithely up to the birds to join them in their rejoicings. But the birds gave him the cold shoulder and flew away. And the beasts gave him exactly the same treatment.

Condemned by both sides and acknowledged by neither, the unhappy bat was obliged to skulk away and live in holes and corners, never caring to show his face except in the dusk of twilight.

&*Application*: HE WINDS UP FRIENDLESS WHO PLAYS BOTH SIDES AGAINST THE MIDDLE.

THE FARMER
AND THE SNAKE

ONE WINTER'S DAY as a farmer was homeward bound from market he found a snake lying half dead with cold by the roadside. Taking compassion on the frozen creature, he placed it under his coat to warm it. Then he hastened home and put the serpent down on the hearth where a cheery fire was blazing.

The children watched it with great interest and rejoiced to see it slowly come to life again. But as one of them knelt down to stroke the reviving snake it raised its head and darted out its fangs and would have stung the child to death. Quickly the farmer seized his matlock and with one stroke cut the serpent in two.

Application: NO GRATITUDE IS TO BE EXPECTED FROM THE WICKED.

216

THE THIEF AND
THE DOG

A THIEF was clambering over the wall when the watchdog began barking.

"Be still," hissed the thief, "I am one of your master's friends."

But the dog kept on growling and barking. Hoping to silence him, the thief reached into a bag and tossed some scraps of food down to the dog.

"No, you don't," snapped the watchdog. "I had my suspicions of you before, but now that you are so free with your gifts I am sure your intentions are evil."

Application: A BRIBE IN HAND BETRAYS MISCHIEF AT HEART.

217

THE TRUMPETER
TAKEN PRISONER

URING A BATTLE, a trumpeter very rashly ventured too near the enemy and was taken prisoner.

"Spare me, good sirs, I beseech you," he begged of his captors. "Do not put me to death. I do not fight. I have never taken a life. I do not even carry any weapon, except this harmless trumpet, which I blow now and then."

"All the more reason why you should die," replied the captors. "While you, yourself, have not the spirit to fight, you stir up the others to do battle and to take the lives of our comrades."

ઠ๛ *Application*: HE WHO INCITES TO STRIFE IS WORSE THAN HE WHO TAKES PART IN IT.

218

THE THREE
TRADESMEN

HE ENEMY stood outside the walls of a certain city. As they brought up their siege
weapons and arranged their forces for the attack,
the desperate defenders within held a council of
war to determine the best means of holding their
city.

A bricklayer arose. "Sirs," said he, "it is my opin-
ion that the best material for this purpose is brick."
Then he sat down.

A carpenter asked to be recognized. "I beg to dif-
fer with the bricklayer. The material that will best
serve our desperate needs is wood. Let timber be our
defense!"

Then a tanner jumped to his feet. "Citizens," he

219

cried, "when you all have had your say, I wish to remind you that there is nothing in the world like leather!"

> *Application*: IT IS DIFFICULT TO SEE BEYOND ONE'S OWN NOSE.

THE SHEPHERD
AND THE SEA

THE GRAZING being poor in the hills, a shepherd moved his flock down near the shore where the sea mists kept the grass fresh and green. As he guarded his sheep he delighted in gazing out over the tranquil sea, so smooth and calm and limitless. One day he was seized with a strong desire to sail over that peaceful expanse of blue water.

So the shepherd sold his flock and received a good price because of the fatness of the sheep. With the money he bought a cargo of dates which he loaded on a vessel and set sail for another port. He had not gone far, however, when the sky became dark and a storm arose. The boat was driven upon the rocks and

221

wrecked, and his cargo of dates and everything he owned was swallowed up by the sea. Indeed, it was only by good fortune that the one-time shepherd was rescued and able to get to land.

Not long after this unhappy experience, the shepherd was sitting sorrowfully on the shore looking out to sea (which now was calm and serene once more) when one of his friends came up to him and said: "I see you are admiring the ocean. How beautiful and tranquil is the sea. Could any vista be more inviting!"

"Have a care, my good fellow," replied the shepherd sourly, "of that smooth surface; it is only looking out for your dates."

ক্ষ *Application*: TRUST NOT IN HIM THAT SEEMS A SAINT.

THE FARMER
AND HIS DOGS

৯ IT WAS the coldest winter within the memory of the oldest living inhabitant. The roads were blocked by snowdrifts so deep that people could not struggle through them. A farmer found himself completely isolated with the drifts piled up to the eaves of his house. When his provisions ran out he was forced to slaughter one of his own sheep for food. Still the bitter weather continued. When all his sheep had been consumed he was forced to eat up his goats. And at last—for there still was no break in that terrible winter—the farmer had to sacrifice his valuable plow oxen to keep his family from starving.

When the dogs observed that the cattle had gone the same way as the sheep and goats they said to one another: "Let us be off, no matter how deep the snow. For if our master has had no pity on the working oxen, how is it likely then that he will spare us?"

৯ *Application*: WHEN OUR NEIGHBOR'S HOUSE IS ON FIRE, IT IS TIME TO LOOK TO OUR OWN.

THE QUACK
FROG

A FROG, emerging from the mud of the swamp, announced to all the animal world that he could cure every manner of disease. Interested to see what all the croaking was about, the animals gathered around, and the frog, more puffed up than ever by the attention he was receiving, bellowed:

"Here, come and see! You are looking upon the greatest physician in all the world. Not even Aesculapius, Jove's court doctor—"

He was interrupted by a loud bray from the jackass. A goat, also, seemed to be somewhat skeptical of the frog's boastings and said so. Then up spoke the fox: "How dare you set up to heal others? Why do you not try first to cure your own limping gait?"

"And your own blotched and wrinkled skin," added the hare.

"And your own bulging and ugly eyes," said the sheep.

At this the quack frog drew in his head and hopped away in the direction of the bog whence he had come while the animals laughed him to scorn.

Application: PHYSICIAN, HEAL THYSELF!

THE BALD KNIGHT

A CERTAIN knight observing himself in the mirror one day noted that he was growing old. His hair no longer grew as luxuriantly upon his head as once it had. Indeed, he had become quite bald. To conceal such a noticeable imperfection he ordered a very handsome periwig.

One day with a group of his friends he went riding to the hounds. He was dressed in his gayest apparel and on his naked pate he wore his brand-new wig. A sudden gust of wind snatched off the knight's toupee, exposing his bald noggin much to the amusement of his companions. He himself laughed as loud as anybody, saying: "How was it to be expected that I should keep someone's else hair upon my head, when my own would not stay there?"

కు *Application*: THY PRIDE IS BUT THE PROLOGUE OF THY SHAME.

THE ASS AND
HIS DRIVER

A FARMER was driving an ass along a country lane on the way to town. The beast bore no burden and was being allowed to amble along at his own gait. Suddenly the idea came to him to leave the beaten track and make for the edge of a precipice which bordered the roadway.

When he was just on the point of falling over, his master ran up and, seizing him by the tail, tried with might and main to pull him back. Willfully the ass resisted, pulling the contrary way. The farmer, seeing that he was about to be pulled over the precipice along with the stubborn beast, let go his hold. As the ass went hurtling over the brink his master cried after him: "Well, Jack, if you will be master, you will have to continue on alone."

Application: A WILLFUL BEAST MUST GO HIS OWN WAY.

228

VENUS AND
THE CAT

ɞ IN ANCIENT TIMES there lived a beautiful cat who fell in love with a young man. Naturally, the young man did not return the cat's affections, so she besought Venus, the goddess of love and beauty, for help. The goddess, taking compassion on her plight, changed her into a fair damsel.

No sooner had the young man set eyes on the maiden than he became enamored of her beauty and in due time led her home as his bride. One evening a short time later, as the young couple were sitting in their chamber, the notion came to Venus to discover whether in changing the cat's form she had also changed her nature. So she set down a mouse before the beautiful damsel. The girl, reverting completely to her former character, started from her seat and pounced upon the mouse as if she would eat it on the spot, while her husband watched her in dismay.

The goddess, provoked by such clear evidence that the girl had revealed her true nature, turned her into a cat again.

ɞ *Application*: WHAT IS BRED IN THE BONE WILL
        NEVER BE ABSENT IN THE FLESH.

229

THE WOLF AND
THE SHEPHERDS

A WOLF chanced to be looking through the doorway of a hut where some shepherds were comfortably regaling themselves upon a joint of mutton. As he heard them smack their lips over the juicy morsels and watched them carving the roasted carcass with their knives, his lips curled with scorn.

Said he to himself: "These shepherds seem mightily pleased with themselves. But what would they do were they to observe me partaking of a similar supper?"

᪲ *Application*: MEN ARE TOO APT TO CONDEMN IN OTHERS THE VERY THINGS THEY DO THEMSELVES.

THE HEDGE AND
THE VINEYARD

 change A FOOLISH young heir came into the possession of his wise father's estate. After the funeral and when his patrimony was securely in his hands, the young man ordered his servants to cut down all of the hedges that surrounded his vineyard. When the servants sought to dissuade their new master from his purpose he shouted: "Why should they not be grubbed up? They bear no grapes; they yield no harvest; they occupy good land that should be planted to vines. Grub them up and burn them."

So the fences were torn down and the vineyard was open to the ravages of man and beast, and it was not long before the vines were all destroyed. And thus the simple fellow learned, when it was too late, that while it is true that one ought not to expect to gather grapes from brambles, yet it is quite as important to protect one's vineyard as to possess it.

change *Application*: THEY ALSO SERVE WHO ONLY STAND AND WAIT.

THE WIDOW
AND THE HEN

A POOR WIDOW living alone in the country kept a faithful hen. Each morning the hen laid a big, brown egg for the woman's breakfast.

One day the widow thought to herself: "Now if I were to double my hen's allowance of barley, she would lay me two eggs a day instead of one." So she started feeding her biddy a double measure of grain, and soon the hen began to grow fat and sleek and lazy. It wasn't long before she stopped laying altogether.

Application: FIGURES DON'T LIE, BUT THEY WON'T MAKE A HEN LAY.

THE STAG AND
THE VINE

᠊ A STAG, pursued by hunters and weary from
the long chase, took refuge among the branches of
a vine where he concealed himself amidst the foliage.
The hunters passed within a few yards of him without discovering his hiding place. As the sound of
their voices died away and the stag thought that all
was safe, he began nibbling at the tender green
leaves that had sheltered him.

As he tugged at the leaves the movement of the
branches caught the attention of one of the hunters.
Guessing at once that his prey was there, the hunter
drew his bow and shot an arrow into the rustling
vine and killed the stag. As the animal lay dying he
groaned: "I am being justly punished for my ingratitude toward the vine that had protected me in time
of danger."

᠊ *Application*: THROW NO STONES INTO THE WELL
THAT QUENCHED YOUR THIRST.

THE BOY
BATHING

෫ IT WAS a warm day in early spring. A boy walking by the bank of a river could not resist the temp-
tation to remove his clothes and plunge in for the
first swim of the year. But the water proved to be
much colder and deeper than it had appeared from
the shore. The boy was on the point of sinking when
he caught sight of a wayfarer strolling along the
shore.

"Help! Help!" screamed the boy. "I am drowning.
Save me!"

Instead of plunging in at once to the lad's rescue,
the traveler called out: "You foolish young man,
don't you realize that this is not the season to go
bathing? What would your mother say if she knew
you were in the river at this time of year? I have a
good mind to report this matter to the authorities.
Whatever were you thinking of—"

"Oh, save me now, sir," interrupted the struggling
boy, "and read me the lecture afterward!"

෫ *Application*: THERE IS A TIME AND PLACE FOR
EVERYTHING.

ALPHABETICAL LIST
OF FABLES

THE BEAUTIFUL
Illustrated Junior Library®
EDITIONS